Cambridge Elements

Elements in the Philosophy of Martin Heidegger
edited by
Filippo Casati
Lehigh University
Daniel O. Dahlstrom
Boston University

HEIDEGGER ON TRANSCENDENCE

Chad Engelland
University of Dallas

Shaftesbury Road, Cambridge CB2 8EA, United Kingdom

One Liberty Plaza, 20th Floor, New York, NY 10006, USA

477 Williamstown Road, Port Melbourne, VIC 3207, Australia

314–321, 3rd Floor, Plot 3, Splendor Forum, Jasola District Centre,
New Delhi – 110025, India

103 Penang Road, #05–06/07, Visioncrest Commercial, Singapore 238467

Cambridge University Press is part of Cambridge University Press & Assessment,
a department of the University of Cambridge.

We share the University's mission to contribute to society through the pursuit of education, learning and research at the highest international levels of excellence.

www.cambridge.org
Information on this title: www.cambridge.org/9781009515986

DOI: 10.1017/9781009516006

When citing this work, please include a reference to the DOI 10.1017/9781009516006

First published 2025

A catalogue record for this publication is available from the British Library

ISBN 978-1-009-51598-6 Hardback
ISBN 978-1-009-51599-3 Paperback
ISSN 2976-5668 (online)
ISSN 2976-565X (print)

Heidegger on Transcendence

Elements in the Philosophy of Martin Heidegger

DOI: 10.1017/9781009516006
First published online: May 2025

Chad Engelland
University of Dallas

Author for correspondence: Chad Engelland, cengelland@udallas.edu

Abstract: *Heidegger on Transcendence* maps the deep ambivalences that attend Heidegger's lasting commitment to the transcendental tradition, construed here broadly to include not only phenomenological but also modern, medieval, and ancient predecessors. It defends Heidegger's commitment by explicating the essential function of the transcendental within his path of thinking and by contextualizing his later comments on transcending the limits of the subject still inherent in the metaphysical language heretofore available to transcendental thought.

Keywords: phenomenology, transcendental philosophy, Martin Heidegger, experience, metaphysics

ISBNs: 9781009515986 (HB), 9781009515993 (PB), 9781009516006 (OC)
ISSNs: 2976-5668 (online), 2976-565X (print)

Contents

Introduction: The *Transzendenzfrage*

Heidegger's preferred metaphors are agrarian and rustic, consisting of countrysides and wooded paths that empty into clearings trodden by peasants ever pursuing their crafts. To transcend then has the sense of a peculiar movement that leads us ever deeper into the thickness of the natural terrain. Supposing we were to transpose Heidegger's metaphorical pattern to the sea (Withy 2015), and go down to the Piraeus, not as a port but as a place of recreation, taking as our reference the surfer? Here to transcend would mean, in the first place, to overcome stasis and to paddle hard in order to catch the wave, and having caught the wave to be carried along by its raw native force. To speak in Heideggerian terms, a certain projection and anticipation is necessary just in order to catch up to the fundamental happening of being appropriated by the swell, which will otherwise pass one by. We speak of "catching" a wave but in fact to catch a wave is a matter of allowing oneself to be caught by the wave, for the wave remains thoroughly beyond one's control. While so caught, all talk of paddling falls out and yet the paddling was not for nothing, because it alone secured the possibility that now renders its further exercise otiose. Surfing is a quintessentially contemplative exercise of cooperating with powers unfathomable to us. The horizon is not something static opposite the surfer but instead that out of which heretofore hidden waves surge (Engelland 2021a). So, from one point of view, Heidegger's transcendence may have been a *Holzweg*, a trail that leads into the depths of the woods, but from another it is the occasion for surfing the surf which surfaces the depths that it simultaneously reveals and conceals. Thought in this way, Heideggerian transcendence is fundamentally akin to the aim of the surfer. It aspires to catch up in thought to the being caught up by experience. To follow it is to experience real and genuine joy, to be stoked, but that is the fruit of much patient waiting, corresponding disappointment, and some real, honest work, crowned by something that can only be counted as a blessing.

With the subject of this book we find Heidegger at a rare, cosmopolitan moment. For he appears most often as a thinker that is quintessentially German with a romantic fondness for everything Greek, and to read him is to again and again find oneself confronted with the idiosyncratic contours of the German and Greek languages. "Only someone who is German can in an originarily new way poetize being and say being – he alone will conquer anew the essence of *theōria* and finally create *logic*" (GA94: 27). But this Germanness counts only to the extent it reconnects to the Greeks (GA94: 101). Given this linguistic parochialism, it is no surprise that when we survey the Heideggerian corpus, we find little engagement with thinkers whose thoughts are expressed in the language of Latin, despite his early competence in medieval philosophy, and, no surprise that, unlike his teacher Husserl, there is no appreciation for or much engagement with philosophers writing in English or French. Accordingly, Heidegger's thought does not translate well, and yet he hints that his one great contribution to philosophy may simply have been to emphasize the significance of the Greek word for truth as unconcealment and thereby to translate it into a contemporary vocabulary (GA77: 99).

During the 1920s, however, under the spell of Husserl, at the specific moment in which *Being and Time* sprang from his pen, the Latin tongue and the authors who wrote in Latin, including not only Augustine but also Thomas Aquinas, had a role in expressing the fundamental motion of thinking that fulfilled the programs of Greek and German philosophy; indeed, the German authors that became privileged interlocutors at the time were not Nietzsche and Hölderlin but Leibniz and Kant, both of whom wrote treatises not only in German but also Latin. Heidegger, the thinker of *Sein* and *alētheia*, deigned to express his topic as *veritas transcendentalis* or *veritas temporalis* and even employed a suite of Latinate terms to correlate with his Germanic vocabulary. To transcend means to step beyond to the horizon of all understanding. As Heidegger saw it, the quest for the a priori unites a disparate band of thinkers from across the continent and across the ages. As they sought the condition for experiencing entities, so Heidegger sought the condition for experiencing being. His was a "transcendental question raised to a higher power" (*potenzierte transzendentale Frage*) (GA82: 352).

Rather than being an accident or detour, Heidegger's cosmopolitan transcendentalism is the heart of his entire philosophy, its point of departure and return.[1] Everything else one might wish to appropriate either prepares for it or attempts to round it out. Subtract transcendentalism from Heidegger and what remains is, to paraphrase Nietzsche, German, all too German, or, in fairness to Germans, just a regionalism or parochialism that from time to time succumbs to what Heidegger in a moment of sobriety chastised as "uninhibited word mysticism" (SZ: 220).[2] My view, by contrast, is that phenomenology liberates the tongue of every language to say what needs to be said about its possibility (Engelland 2021b).

This reading of the prominence of the transcendental was once controversial. But it need no longer be so now that we can array the hundred plus volumes of

[1] For the phrase, "Heidegger's Transcendentalism," I am indebted to Dahlstrom 2005.

[2] At the start of the 1931 lecture course, Heidegger quotes a passage from Nietzsche's *Will to Power* claiming the inner kinship of German and Greek thinking (GA 33: 1/xvi). In the lecture, he censures the transcendental philosophy of the medievals as being nothing but a tomb of propositions (GA 33: 32/26). He does not renounce Kant, though he no longer views him as an ally but instead as a distant prelude (GA33: 33/27). Heidegger's cosmopolitan moment was over.

the *Gesamtausgabe* before us and apprehend so unambiguously and unmistakably Heidegger's unwavering commitment to transcendentalism. He himself again and again attests to the centrality of the transcendental on two points: for joining his path of thinking and for making sense of further progress on that path. For example, he writes, "One might hold that the 'transcendental' way through *Being and Time* is superfluous. Whoever thinks thus runs the danger [*Gefahr*] of holding that the thinking after the turn is a speculative stroll [*Spaziergang*] according to which one appears still only to poetize [*dichtet*]" (GA82: 403). Now poetize here does not mean in the first place to write poetry but instead the mode of comportment that follows from *technē* and which operates in phenomenological fashion in order to lead something forth. But without the transcendental as a lasting reference point Heidegger cannot distinguish the philosophical from the poetic logos. Transcendentalism, rather than being superfluous, delivers over to him his lasting subject matter and enables a philosophical articulation of that domain. Heidegger continues the passage: "Whereas *Alētheia* as such first becomes worthy of thought. But the bindingness of the corresponding thinking can first then become discussed, when the matter which binds is first adequately shown, in which the 'logic' of *this* thinking as reflection on language becomes a task" (GA82: 403). Only the transcendentalism of *Being and Time* leads us today into the place of thinking, and only by appreciating the astounding success of the transcendentalism of *Being and Time* can we register the fact that the poetic mode of the later thinking is intended to be nothing more than a *more adequate* saying of the self-same philosophical domain.

With this sort of evidence available, what "one says," namely that Heidegger abandons transcendentalism, is no longer defensible. His criticisms of transcendentalism, which abound at every stage of his thinking, including the very works in which he most enthusiastically identifies with it, do not constitute a disavowal; Heidegger is careful, at times pedantically so, to qualify all criticisms of the transcendentalism of *Being and Time* so that the basic transcendental movement of the text remains in force. In his view, transcendentalism is the *sine qua non* of making the thinker to be a thinker and, in my view, it is the *sine qua non* of making this thinker to be one worth thinking about. For it is the transcendental Heidegger that is not an obscurantist or mere poet; he is one that can enter into conversation with other philosophers, including contemporary ones, concerning normativity and meaning (Crowell and Malpas 2007; Crowell 2013; Golob 2014; Engelland 2015; Engelland 2020b; Burch and McMullin 2020). The transcendental Heidegger helps us open our eyes to see and our ears to hear the presencing and absencing of things and, accordingly, also presencing and absencing itself.

The transcendentalism of the ancients and the moderns approaches entities in terms of being. Heidegger's transcendentalism is a transcendentalism squared that approaches being in terms of time as the transcendental horizon. In his first pass over the terrain, he hazards a more projective disclosure of the transcendental domain in terms of research into the a priori. In his second pass over the same terrain, he works out a more affective disclosure of the transcendental domain in terms of the attunement of fundamental moods. Perhaps in his shifting talk of the transcendental Heidegger had in mind his medieval training in a kind of "*via negationis et eminentiae*" (cf. SZ: 427). The cataphatic affirmation of sameness with the transcendental tradition passes through an apophatic moment of denial before finally realizing a mode of super-eminent affirmation. What transcendentalism always groped for in its clumsy way is finally achieved in Heidegger's own thinking, shorn of inappropriate modes of reflection and residual commitments to consciousness (cf. Herrmann 2022). Heidegger affirms the basis of transcendence, denies the associations inappropriate to it, and affirms – in a higher mode – terms appropriate to its terminus.

The Paradox of Novelty

Here is the dilemma facing Heidegger and thus the dilemma facing us, his interpreters. On the one hand, as he puts it in 1923, "We stand before completely new tasks that have nothing to do with traditional philosophy" (GA17: 1). Heidegger is aware that his horizon of questioning does not match that of the philosophical tradition, and hence there is no existing vocabulary to say what he thinks needs to be said. On the other hand, pick up any of his books, essays, and lecture courses, and see that Heidegger expends most of his energies interpreting, productively, figures in the history of philosophy while appropriating their operative vocabularies. This procedure presumably aims to reproduce, for his interlocutor, the very engagement with the tradition that led him to a topic that transcends the traditional horizon of inquiry and its existing vocabulary. Heidegger thus offers us, repeatedly, ambivalent readings of key figures, who are alternatively lauded and censured. Yet how can this tradition offer any help in opening up his topic if his topic has "nothing to do with traditional philosophy"?

Heidegger happens upon an image to make sense of the paradox. He who wishes to make a great leap forward must go a great deal back (GA94: 234).[3] In this case, Heidegger does not merely wish to step beyond or transcend the tradition; he wishes to leap beyond the horizon of its beginning to another beginning and horizon for thinking. But, just in order to effect the novelty, he

[3] The image can be found in Nietzsche's *Beyond Good and Evil*, §280.

must find, in the first beginning, momentum forward. Heidegger wishes to prepare for the leap by appropriating the highpoint of the tradition, namely the theme of transcendence. The preparation for the leap is transcendence's movement of stepping beyond. Heidegger, in other words, will accomplish the primary movement of his thinking by means of wielding transcendence against transcendence, of leaping beyond the stepping beyond of things.

Now, one often reasons that if Heidegger were a philosopher, he must be one that seeks to clarify the age-old question of being, and hence the first word in the title of his breakthrough text, *Being and Time*. And if he employs a method it would be hermeneutical phenomenology rather than transcendental thinking (Schalow 2020). Yet he does not seek being simpliciter but rather the *meaning* of being, and the meaning of being is arrived at by exhibiting the transcendental horizon of temporality. What comes to the fore in Heidegger is the problem of the unity of the many senses of being, up to and including the relatedness of being to the human being. By consequence, if it makes sense to think of Heidegger as a thinker of being and its interpretation, it makes even more sense to think of him as a transcendental thinker who remains focused on the various kinds of transcendence and their interrelation. The magnum opus indicates this focus in the title's "*and Time*." Heidegger aims to interpret timeliness, phenomenologically elucidated as ecstatic and horizonal, as the condition for the possibility of understanding being, and in this capacity he terms it temporality. The meaning of being is the transcendental horizon of temporality. If Heidegger seeks being, he does so transcendentally. If phenomenology, inflected hermeneutically, names his method, transcendence names his subject matter as the dynamic movement of thought's coming back to its own origins in being *and* time.

What gave rise to this breakthrough text, *Being and Time*? Heidegger's way of interpreting the tradition motivates his new program by means of highlighting a certain family resemblance among a variety of thinkers, including Plato, Aristotle, Aquinas, Leibniz, Kant, and Husserl. All of them contributed to varying degrees to the general program of advancing the question of being through a renewed sense of the being of relatedness, up to and including the marvelous relatedness of the open being of the human and the manifest being of things. The highpoint of this tradition is the introduction of time as the transcendental horizon for making sense of things. Heidegger fashions a new synthesis of the transcendental, one which transcends the opposition of the ancients and the moderns, and therein lies his determinate significance for philosophy (Dahlstrom 2005; Tate 2015; Engelland 2017).

Heidegger is a thinker of dynamic movement and therefore the vocabulary of stepping beyond or transcendence recommends itself. The basic idea of transcendence is to step beyond relative to a retreating horizon, but transcendence also names how such stepping beyond is possible, both on the side of the one that transcends and on the side of that which is transcended.

> Transcendence means surpassing [*Überstieg*]. That which accomplishes such surpassing and dwells in this surpassing is transcendent (transcending). As an occurrence, this surpassing pertains to something that is. Formally speaking, surpassing may be grasped as a "relation" that passes "from" something "to" something. To surpassing there thus belongs that *toward which* such surpassing occurs, that which is usually, though inaccurately, called the "transcendent." And finally, there is in each case *something* that is surpassed in this surpassing. These moments are taken from a "spatial" occurrence to which the expression "transcendence" initially refers. (GA9: 137/107)

Heidegger exposes us to the interconnected tissue of transcendence. The fundamental structure of *Being and Time* was to move from transcending things (SZ 1.1) through transcendence as such (SZ 1.2) to time as determining transcendence (SZ 1.3). What complicates this picture is that transcendence appears to name only the way up rather than also the way down; that is, it projects being in terms of time rather than showing how time engenders being. Heidegger accordingly replaces the unilateral movement of stepping with the reciprocal movement of swinging, and, correlatively, he emphasizes that all transcendental projection of the understanding takes its bearing from a prior affective displacement into a horizon of understanding. The horizon is not projected but disclosed. Our aim now is not to go beyond or to limit such going beyond, but instead to learn to abide more intensely within the reciprocal belonging of self and being. How does he come to express his philosophical project in terms of the movement of transcending? What event enables him to find help in this tradition of thinking?

Heidegger's Damascus Moment: The Husserl–Kant–Heidegger Alliance

On the last day of the 1927–28 lecture course, Heidegger wrote: "Several years ago as I studied anew the *Critique of Pure Reason*, and read it as it were against the backdrop of Husserl's phenomenology, the scales fell from my eyes, and Kant became for me confirmation of the correctness of the way for which I was seeking" (GA25: 431, trans. modified). Heidegger's biblical language here is striking. After the experience on the road to Damascus, scales fell from the eyes of Saint Paul (Acts 9:18), who had previously been persecuting the Christians. Heidegger, like Saint Paul, now advocates the very position he had been burying. The event occurs during the 1925–26 lecture course. Mid-semester, Heidegger abandons his Aristotelian schema and begins enthusiastically interpreting Kant. How does Husserl give him the optics to read Kant in such a way that the result confirms *Heidegger's* own approach?

The semester before, in 1925, Heidegger wrote out a draft of *Being and Time* as the fulfilment of Husserl's notion of phenomenological research, that is, an investigation of the a priori condition for the possibility of intentionality through categorial and hermeneutical articulation. Two things are noteworthy about this text. First, Heidegger, though critical of Husserl's neglect of being, is suddenly again quite positive about phenomenology as a program of research into the a priori. "Even today I still regard myself as a learner in relation to Husserl" (GA20: 168). What prompted this change of heart from previous Marburg lecture courses? On February 7, 1925, Husserl sent Heidegger a copy of the manuscript for *Ideas II*.[4] Heidegger writes of the development in terms of a new focus on the *Zusammenhang* as such: "The main point now is not to view the context of lived experience as an appendage to physical things but to see that experiential context as such and the ego as a psychic ego-subject" (GA20: 168). Second, Heidegger remains thoroughly opposed to Kant, dismissing his investigation of the a priori as (1) epistemological rather than metaphysical and (2) relegated to the subjective sphere, subscribing to the "old mythology of an intellect which glues and rigs together the world's matter with its own forms" (GA20: 96). On both counts, Kantianism is thoroughly refuted by phenomenology (GA20: 100–103).

Returning to the question of Heidegger's Damascus moment, we can say that the Husserl of *Ideas II* gives Heidegger a program of research into the experiential context as such, an understanding that Heidegger at first could not attribute to Kant but later does beginning in the 1925–26 lecture course; this Husserlian Kant in turn goes further than Husserl himself in collaborating with Heidegger's own program. Kant confirms, that is, his philosophizing fulfils the very meaning-intention inscribed in Heidegger's own approach. As Heidegger writes in 1926, "In the modern period, Kant became a Greek of the first rank, if only for a short time" (GA22: 313/230). We have therefore three transcendental philosophies: (1) Husserl's transcendental phenomenology, which enables Heidegger to appreciate (2) Kant's transcendental philosophy, which confirms (3) Heidegger's own transcendentalism, a transcendentalism that germinated while both Husserl and Kant were held at arm's length.

In another publication, I detail Heidegger's relation to the transcendentalism of Husserl and of Kant (Engelland 2017). Here I focus on Heidegger's own transcendentalism, which owes its original form to the Aristotelian-Thomistic tradition of metaphysics. Aristotle, who regards the soul as potentially all things, thinks things are made manifest via perception and intellection;

[4] On the significance of this text for the course, see Theodore Kisiel (2002: 38).

Thomas, working out truth as a transcendental property of being, says that each thing is true insofar as the intellective soul can "come together with" (*convenire cum*) it (SZ: 14). The original sense of transcendence is this coming together of the soul with all things.

Heidegger's philosophical voice was set free by an intuition or hunch that the metaphysical language of essence was equivalent to the transcendental language of condition for the possibility and that both were determined as a peculiar modality of time, the *a priori perfect tense* (SZ: 441). Operating on this hunch, he plunged forward into sweeping phenomenological analyses of the subjectivity of the subject in order to lay bare the condition for the possibility of experience in the structure of the finite agent of experience.

Heidegger's 1928 moment of retrospection concerning his Kant conversion comes just as he is about to advance a further stage of his transcendental project. Not only is time the horizon of being; with Leibniz and Kant, Heidegger pioneers a metaphysics of transcendence that will culminate in "On the Essence of Ground" and *Kant and the Problem of Metaphysics*. It is this second stage of his transcendentalism that he will later come to regret but only insofar as his first stage remains in play.

We have thus three interconnected events. First, there is a renewed fidelity to Husserl's phenomenology in 1925 thanks to working through the unpublished manuscript for *Ideas II*, a fidelity that yielded what Theodore Kisiel (2002: 39) dubbed "a pure phenomenological draft" of *Being and Time* in the summer 1925 lecture course; Kant, however, remains outside of the phenomenological camp. Second, through Husserl's phenomenology, specifically its sense of making-present and its program of philosophical research, there is a phenomenological Kant, who everywhere relates all philosophical issues back to time as their horizon of understanding; it is for this reason that *Being and Time* adopts a transcendental vocabulary. Third, in 1928, Heidegger works out with Leibniz the key to undermining the neo-Kantian epistemological reading of Kant, which culminates in "On the Essence of Ground" and the 1929 *Kant and the Problem of Metaphysics*; here the heart of a philosophical work is its function as a metaphysical ground-laying. This third event yields his most intensive and extensive deployment of the vocabulary of transcendental philosophy, a deployment that brings about the fulfilment of the phenomenological program of returning to the things themselves.

How are we to think of these three? It is as though Husserl's gift of the *Ideas II* manuscript fertilizes the soil, giving Heidegger a renewed sense of phenomenology as concerned with making present the conditions of experiencing being, and such a fertile soil leads Heidegger to recognize in Kant, against the prevailing neo-Kantian reading, a more vital collaborator in this Husserlian project. Finally, this leads to what Heidegger then regards as the full flowering of this possibility in the metaphysics of transcendence. Heidegger does not become Kantian, but Kant becomes Heideggerian. As Dahlstrom (1991) comments, "Perhaps what is most remarkable about Heidegger's interpretation is the way in which he thus attempts to *desubjectify* the notions of time and self-affection as they are presented by Kant" (359).

Heidegger later speaks of the Kant book itself as a kind of "refuge" (*Zuflucht*) from which he sought to defend the legitimacy of the transcendentalism of *Being and Time* from its early critics (GA3: xiv). Yet, though he retracts the book as an adequate interpretation of *Kant*'s horizon of questioning, he continues to propose it as a clarification of the project of *Being and Time*. Heidegger's transcendentalism is not the refuge from the storm of criticism; the refuge is rather the authority of Kant, under the spell of the earlier conversion. Yet Heidegger never, even at his most enthusiastic moment, regards Kant's transcendentalism as synonymous with his own. Nor does he ever identify the heritage of the transcendental tradition with Kant, since it has classical, medieval, and contemporary non-Kantian representatives. Kantian subjectivism is not the last or only word on transcendentalism. Heidegger's non-subjective transcendentalism survives as a transcendentalism despite its eventual disassociation from its Kantian precursor. See Table 1.

Heidegger's Transcendentalism

Heidegger's transcendentalism is characterized by a peculiar way of speaking. It deploys talk of "making possible" and specifies "conditions for the possibility" often in the form of a string of "only if" or "only because" propositions. As he writes in "What Is Metaphysics?":

> Only because the nothing is manifest in the ground of human existence can the total strangeness of entities overwhelm us. Only when the strangeness of entities oppresses us does it arouse and evoke wonder. Only on the ground of wonder – the manifestness of the nothing – does the "why?" loom before us. Only because the "why" is possible as such can we in a definite way inquire into grounds and ground things. Only because we can question and ground things is the destiny of our existence placed in the hands of the researcher. (GA9: 121/95–96)

These conditions target transcendence: "If in the ground of its essence human existence were not transcending, which now means, if it were not in advance holding itself out into the nothing, then it could never adopt a stance toward entities nor even toward itself" (GA9: 115/91). As he writes in his *Festschrift* contribution for Husserl, such transcendence enables experience: "If one

Table 1 Some species of transcendental philosophy

	Species	Question	Movement of thought
T^1	Kant	How are synthetic judgments possible a priori?	A critique of pure reason
	Husserl	How is constitution possible in terms of time?	An exhibition of transcendental intersubjectivity in its a priori
	Heidegger SZ 1.1–2	How must we be to be open to the self-showing of entities?	An analytic of timely human existence
T^2	Heidegger, SZ 1.3, version a (*affective-projective*)	How does the interplay of presence and absence let being be?	An authentic analytic of temporality in its a priori perfect tense
	Heidegger, SZ 1.3, version b (as principally *projective*)		A metaphysical ground-laying of the essence of experience
	Heidegger, SZ 1.3, version c (as principally *affective*)		The appropriation of human existence by the matter-to-be-thought

characterizes all *comportment* toward entities as intentional, then *intentionality* is possible only *on the grounds of transcendence*" (GA9: 135/106). Or again:

> "Human existence transcends" means: in the essence of its being it is *world-forming*, "forming" [*bildend*] in the multiple sense that it lets world occur, and through the world gives itself an original view (form [*Bild*]) that is not explicitly grasped, yet functions precisely as a paradigmatic form [*Vor-bild*] for all manifest entities, among which each respective human existence itself belongs (GA9: 158/123).

Such transcendental agency is premised on the genuine alterity of things and is in service to their self-disclosure:

> Only if, amid entities in their totality, entities come to be "more in being" in the manner of temporalizing of human existence are there the hours and days of entities' entry into the world. And only if this primordial history, namely, transcendence, occurs, i.e., only if being having the character of being-in-the-world irrupt into entities, is there the possibility of entities manifesting themselves (GA9: 159/123).

How does the condition-for-the-possibility talk of these 1929 essays relate to the project of *Being and Time*? He explains:

> What has been published so far of the investigations on "Being and Time" has no other task than that of a concrete projection unveiling *transcendence* (Cf. §§ 12–83; especially § 69). This in turn occurs for the purpose of enabling the *sole* guiding intention, clearly indicated in the *title* of the *whole* of Part I, of attaining the "*transcendental* horizon of the *question* concerning being." All concrete interpretations, above all that of time, are to be evaluated *solely* in the perspective of *enabling* the *question* of being (GA9: 162n59/371).

Thus Heidegger clarifies that the purpose of his phenomenological analyses is to work out the condition for the possibility of experiencing being. What the singled-out §69 gives us is Heidegger's reply to neo-Kantianism, which posits forms that confect experience. Heidegger's phenomenology of transcendence, by contrast, discloses the contours of experience in terms of the horizon from which we return in making sense of things.

> Thus the significance-relationships which determine the structure of the world are not a network of forms which a wordless subject has laid over some kind of material. What is rather the case is that factical human existence, understanding itself and its world ecstatically in the unity of the "there", comes back from these horizons to the entities encountered within them (SZ: 396/417).

At the heart of *Being and Time*, then, is a transcendental science of phenomenological ontology, which sorts and relates the various senses of transcendence: "*Being is the transcendens pure and simple.* And the transcendence of human existence's being is distinctive in that it implies the possibility and the necessity of the most radical *individuation*. Every disclosure of being as the *transcendens* is *transcendental* knowledge. *Phenomenological truth (the disclosedness of being) is veritas transcendentalis*" (SZ: 38/62). Or again:

> The "problem of transcendence" cannot be brought round to the question of how a subject comes out to an Object, where the aggregate of Objects is identified with the idea of the world. Rather we must ask: what makes it ontologically possible for entities to be encountered within-the-world and Objectified as so encountered? This can be answered by recourse to the transcendence of the world – a transcendence with an ecstatico-horizonal foundation (SZ: 366/417–18).

Table 2 Senses of transcendence

	Transcendental item	*Transcendental movement*
1	Things	Self-showing
2	Being	Affording the context beyond and for the self-showing of things
3	Human existence	Coming back from the horizon of world to the self-showing of things
4	Temporal horizon of being	Casting manifold contexts of being for the self-showing of things

Heidegger's transcendentalism is the ecstatic and horizonal inquiry into the temporal genesis of the experience of being. The transcendental interplay of presence and absence establishes the context in which we can make sense of things. See Table 2.

Heidegger's intensive engagement with transcendentalism comprises what is arguably his most productive period, which yielded not only his magnum opus, *Being and Time*, as well as the only other monograph published in his lifetime, *Kant and the Problem of Metaphysics*, but also some of his most significant essays, such as "On the Essence of Ground" and "What Is Metaphysics?" as well as a series of highly elaborated, phenomenologically rich lecture courses, including *Basic Problems of Phenomenology* (summer semester 1927) and *Fundamental Concepts of Metaphysics* (winter semester 1929–30). If we were to subtract these publications from Heidegger, he would be known principally as a philosophical essayist, with a penchant for meditative and often oracular pronouncements, rather than an original philosophical mind whose investigations illumine some of the most elusive issues in all of philosophy.

Preview

"The lasting element in thinking is the way. And ways of thinking hold within them that mysterious quality that we can walk them forward and backward, and that indeed only the way back will lead us forward" (GA12: 94/12). To do justice to the central place of transcendentalism in Heidegger's path of thinking, the study will proceed in reverse chronological order. Doing so will undercut the scholarly presumption of development, as though there were some sense of progress in his path of thinking, and lead instead toward a more essential encounter with the issues themselves. "Philosophers not only don't go forwards, they don't just tread in place either; rather, they go backwards" (GA77: 21).

The first section, "The Critique of Transcendence," tracks what Heidegger regards as the limits of transcendentalism in terms of problems attending to its tradition as well as the terms "objectivity" and "horizon." Thanks to the success of his transcendentalism he is able to move beyond it in a way that he had not anticipated. It covers the later writings back to 1930.

The second section, "The Metaphysics of Transcendence," presents Heidegger's Aristotelian and Leibnizian reading of Kant's investigation of the condition for the possibility of experience as constituting an investigation of the essence of experience. It includes writings from 1928 and 1929.

The third section, "The Transcendence of Being," turns to the transcendental reciprocity in Heidegger's novel transcendental investigations of time as the horizon for making sense of the various ways in which we speak of being. It includes writings from 1925 through 1928.

The fourth section, "The Transcendence of Things," examines Heidegger's renewal of the traditional transcendental reciprocity of experience and things and the normativity and realism at work in the reciprocity. It likewise concerns the writings from 1925 through 1928.

The fifth, concluding section, "Appropriating Transcendence," takes a step back to focus on the transcendental experience of the between and its continued vitality and possible ramifications. It concerns us now and what we might yet gain from retrieving Heidegger's ecstatic and horizonal project.

The coda glosses a poem by the English poet Gerard Manley Hopkins in Heideggerian terms to illustrate the cosmopolitan character of Heidegger's transcendentalism.

1 The Critique of Transcendence

To critique, Heidegger tells us, carries the positive meaning of determining what is essential: It "means 'to separate,' 'to sort out,' and so 'to bring out the particular.' This setting something apart from others emerges from an elevation [of something] to a new order of rank" (GA41: 121; cf. GA20: 168). In the 1930s through the 1960s, Heidegger regularly subjects the transcendentalism of *Being and Time* to critique in this precise sense. Such a reflection does not comprise a rejection but instead a movement toward completion, a completion that can occur by means of making a fresh start on the ground achieved and cleared by his transcendentalism. To transcend entities in terms of being yields to dwelling with being itself. The terminus of transcendental movement is a rigorously enforced immanent rest at the very point where the transcendental *relata*, being and human existence, meet.

To criticize also means to highlight the flaws or shortcomings of something. But on this score Heidegger is much more worried about what *Being and Time* can *seem* to say rather than what it does say. Even a reader as astute as Lee Braver, for example, puts the fundamental defect of the work as follows: "Within the transcendental framework of *Being and Time*, we autonomically create the clearing much the way Kant's transcendental subject does. There is a constant emphasis there on Dasein as initiating, laying out the conditions for the possibility of experiencing particular kinds of beings that cannot be had simply by passively receiving experience" (Braver 2015: 72). Heidegger, however, never thought we create the clearing even if there is a constant emphasis on human existence's agency in making sense of things (GA24: 421; Polt 2015: 220, 231; Sheehan 2015a: 275). From the start, in the telegraphed turn from projecting being upon time to time's engendering being, there was a fundamental difference between Heidegger's transcendentalism and this version of Kant's. In this regard, Polt helpfully distinguishes between two transcendentalisms, a subjectivist (the typical way of reading Kant) and a "nonsubjectivist" one, which he ascribes to Heidegger:

> My claim is that Heidegger never subscribed to such subjectivism, but instead developed a nonsubjectivist type of transcendental thought in *Being and Time*. The horizonal schemata of time serve as conditions of experience, but they are not products of Dasein's activity; instead, time *happens to* Dasein, so to speak. We find ourselves constituted by temporal ecstases that operate on a level more basic than any subjective activity. To discover the temporality that enables all experience is not to set ourselves up as the creators of being, but to understand how we are temporally drawn into transcendence—into our condition as those who understand being and beings (Polt 2015: 232).

The defect of *Being and Time*, then, was not in Heidegger's supposed idealism or anthropologism but in the unwanted appearance of idealism or anthropologism (GA82: 395; Kraatz 2022a: 518). That is, the defect was principally not the transcendentalism but its inherited baggage which proved to be an obstacle to the reader. In fact, Heidegger pens marginal comments in his copy of *Being and Time* that his transcendence of ecstatic-timeliness temporality moves in the direction of Husserlian phenomenology rather than the "transcendental-philosophical direction of Kantian critical idealism" (SZ: 440). Polt, accordingly, locates the real shortcoming of transcendentalism in its commitment to the ahistorical a priori (Polt 2015: 235–36). I would put it as follows: The way to the clearing takes as its point of departure how things appear to us now; by traversing the way we can then see that how things appear to us now (say in terms of modern *mathesis universalis*) has no ultimate necessity. Or, as Heidegger puts it, temporal appearance and nonappearance yields to historical revealing and concealing: "Not only the appearing and non-appearing 'of being' but also the revealing and concealing is being itself – as appropriation" (GA82: 369). Braver

(2015) is thus right to present the shift as at least in part a move from a "given horizon" to the "givenness of horizons," but this I would argue involves a broadening of the inquiry and mode of access into transcendental conditions rather than its overcoming. Heidegger's transcendentalism, rather than what people think about Kant's or even Husserl's, finds its completion in the hiddenness of the clearing; it is not annulled but fulfilled. "The change of transcendence in the turn—the turn as appropriated in appropriation" (GA82: 369).

From Monologue to Dialogue

In *Ideas* I, Husserl writes: "The transition into pure consciousness through the method of the transcendental reduction necessarily leads rather to the question of the ground of the facticity, now affording itself, of the respective, constituting consciousness" (2014: 106–7). The phenomenological theme of transcendence leads to the question of ground. In 1929, Heidegger rejected Edith Stein's contribution to Husserl's *Festschrift*, because it was written as a dialogue between Husserl and Thomas Aquinas; she resubmitted it lightly edited as a dialectical essay on the question of decentering the transcendental subject through medieval thought. While Heidegger's own contribution to the *Festschrift* was a thoroughgoing development of the foundational significance of the transcendental, Stein instead sought to limit its scope: "[Thomas's] ontology, which attributes to every spiritual being its specific activity, surely has ample room for these constitutive investigations. But it cannot assign a 'foundational' [*'grundlegende'*] meaning to them" (Stein 2014a: 130).

In 1931, Stein shared with Heidegger the typescript to *Potency and Act* in which she develops her confrontation between Husserl and Thomas, arguing that in place of transcendental idealism, we should have a posture of fundamental openness maintained by releasement (*zu-gelassen*) toward ultimate transcendence (Stein, 2009: 409).[5] As Stein labored away on her manuscript through the summer of that year, Heidegger delivered a lecture course on potency and act in Aristotle. His goal was to present a connection between the German and Greek world that would bypass the medieval tradition, which had on his view turned Aristotle's inquiry into a set of lifeless propositions. "The consequences of this complete covering over of the inner source which forms the basis of Aristotle's philosophy and ancient philosophy in general are still evident in Kant, even though it is he who tries to retrieve a genuine – though not

[5] In January 1931, Stein was in Freiburg seeking employment, and Heidegger encouraged her to apply with the Catholic member of the faculty, Martin Honecker, as her sponsor. She spent much of the spring and summer writing a manuscript, *Potency and Act*, with Honecker and Heidegger as the intended audience. Due to the eroding economic situation, the position fell through, but Stein sent the typescript to them in September and, in December 1931, met with Heidegger in Freiburg.

original – meaning for the aforementioned teaching of scholastic philosophy" (GA33: 32/26). Heidegger stands behind the violent interpretation of Kant advanced in the two-year-old Kant book:

> Kant knows only one alternative: to trace these determinations and relationships back to formal logic. However, if Kant is not understood in the way the Kantians understand him, and if one bears in mind that for Kant the original unity of transcendental apperception was the pinnacle of logic, and if this unity is not left simply hanging in the air but is questioned as to its own roots, then it can indeed be shown that and how Kant for the first time since Aristotle was once again starting to broach the real question about being (GA33: 33/27).

In December 1931, Stein and Heidegger talked for over two hours about *Potency and Act*, her manuscript developing the interplay of Thomism and Husserl. She found the conversation "very stimulating and fruitful," and Heidegger, for his part, asked to hold on to the manuscript longer (Stein 2014b: 313).

Fifteen years after the *Festschrift* editorialship, in 1944–45, Heidegger will pen his own dialogue on decentering the transcendental subject. That dialogue involves a trio of characters who walk along a trail and seek the essence of thinking. The three characters – a scholar, a scientist, and a guide – are not so much separate people as three moments of one solitary thinker: The scholar brings to bear the past, the scientist prizes the clarity of present experience, and the guide points enigmatically forward toward a thought that has yet to be formulated. The dialogue advances the paradoxical task of willing nonwilling as the antidote to the modern thinking and modern technology that imposes a transcendental horizon of objectivity on nature. The antidote proves to be *Gelassenheit*, or releasement into the open-region, a term that Heidegger adopts from the thirteenth century Dominican, Meister Eckhart, singled out for praise in the 1931 lecture course for denying the predicate "being" of God and thereby avoiding the problem of analogy (GA33: 46/38). There is no better form than a dialogue for expressing the irruption of otherness and the limits of one's own horizon.

Heidegger's dialogue adopts several motifs from Stein's. First, he adopts the appropriateness of challenging the horizon of the transcendental in dialogical form; just as Stein challenged the completeness of Husserl's transcendentalism, so Heidegger challenges the completeness of his own. Second, he also accepts the limited legitimacy of constitution while denying its groundlaying status; it is necessary as a first step but cannot comprise the last. Third, he too looks toward the premodern and specifically the medieval tradition for an alternative manner of thinking that does not accord a central role to the human subject. The difference, of course, remains: Stein's alternative to transcendentalism involves the vertical dimension of the divine; Heidegger's alternative remains within the horizontal.[6] Put differently, Stein remains a thinker of divine transcendence; Heidegger remains a thinker of ontological transcendence alone.

In fidelity to that transcendence, Heidegger gropes for a new vocabulary to express it. Why? The dialogue provides some enigmatic clues.

The Setting of the Horizon

The phrase "transcendental horizon" in the title for SZ I.3 expresses the deepest theme of Heidegger's transcendentalism. "Horizon" surfaced as a critical term in Husserl's phenomenology demarcating as it does the line between presence and absence: Every perceptual object, for example, necessarily presents horizons of possible further exploration (Husserl 1977: 45). Heidegger's transcendentalism involves sketching the contours of experience, the ultimate horizons for making sense of the being of things. The term further recommends itself to Heidegger: If "transcendence" is Latin, "horizon" is Greek, and it is connected with the very mode of Greek inquiry into the essence of things, the mode in which things are demarcated as the very things they are. What Heidegger glimpsed with Kant and Husserl is the horizon of temporality as the horizon for making sense of being.

In the dialogue, he says the open-region "veils itself as horizon" (GA77: 121). Heidegger's worry is that by importing the term horizon to the domain of experience one in effect makes it appear that, just as the object is only an object when cast against the perception of a perceiver, so the field of experience is only the field of experience when cast over against an agent of experience. But the conditionality is reverse: Only by being cast into the field of experience can the experiencer experience and in turn cast things. The horizon determines human existence rather than human existence determining the horizon.

In this way, the critique of transcendental philosophy is connected with the concept of horizon, which can give the impression that it is stands open due to the activity of the subject. In fact, it constitutes the condition for the possibility of the subject or what Heidegger calls the subjectivity of the subject (Sheehan 2015a: 274–75).

---

[6] In the *Black Notebooks*, Heidegger gives a further reason for distancing himself from transcendentalism: Its language is historically bound to thoughts of transcending the world toward God as the transcendent ground (GA94: 50, 73, 341). For Heidegger's polemic against Christianity in the *Black Notebooks*, see Holger Zaborowski (2016).

Kant's Transcendentalism

In the dialogue, Heidegger restricts "transcendental philosophy" to Kant's horizon of questioning (T^1), which he regards as a distant anticipation of the horizon of questioning achieved in *Being and Time* (T^2). Every philosopher, Heidegger muses, thinks by virtue of emphasizing some key term. Kant's significance consists in the word "transcendence" – he "merely assigned to this word an especially emphatic usage" (GA77: 99). The result is that not only does the thinker say more with a word than is meant in its ordinary usage; the thinker says more than he can fathom: "The thinker even says more than he himself can know, such that he is surprised and above all surpassed by the inexhaustibility of his own word" (GA77: 100).

Heidegger underscores the limitedness of Kant's language of horizon. "What has the character of a horizon is thus only the side turned toward us of a surrounding open, an open which is filled with outward views into outward looks of what to our representing appear as objects" (GA77: 112). But what of the open in itself? We must relate to it as other than another object (GA77: 113). When we do so we discover that it withdraws and, in withdrawing, lets us draw near things without those things standing over against us as objects (GA77: 114). Hence there results in the terminus of Kant's transcendentalism, a decided ambiguity of a contradictory movement of arriving and not yet arriving: "But nevertheless we are in the open-region as we, representing transcendentally, step out into the horizon. And yet again we are not in the open-region, so far as we have not yet let ourselves be involved in it itself as the open-region" (GA77: 121). The very success of the transcendental, in delivering us to the region, at the same time makes possible a more radical appropriation of the region.

Heideggerian Transcendentalism

Heidegger never identified his own transcendentalism with a Kantian inquiry into the condition for the possibility of objectivity. Even though Heidegger in the dialogue grants that that was Kant's horizon of questioning (T^1), it does not affect in any way Heidegger's own very different transcendentalism (T^2). What transpires, however, seems to be this. When Heidegger soberly realizes that Kant's horizon of questioning does not match his own, he jettisons transcendental terminology as prone to confusion. But for our purposes this is not what is decisive. We want to know what becomes of *Heidegger's transcendentalism*, not his transcendental terminology. Does anything of Heidegger's critique of (Kantian) transcendentalism touch upon the transcendentalism of *Being and Time*?

At the heart of his transcendentalism was always a sense of movement, of going beyond in order to come back. In this way, we can discern, in this critique of Kantian transcendence, something of the critique of Heidegger's own transcendental movement. World and horizon do not stand open opposite our activity; rather only because the open-region is first open can we subsequently come back to ourselves and others. "Releasement, as the releasing of oneself from transcendental representing, is in fact a refraining from the willing of a horizon" (GA77: 142). Instead of willing to step beyond, Heidegger offers a posture of releasement into the region in which things can be met with. In the place of *Being and Time*'s authenticity of the researcher, there is a new emphasis on our affectivity.

Yet why all the insistence on horizon as outward look? Did Heidegger ever adopt that as his own view? In 1926, while *Being and Time* was in press, he says, "Philosophical truth is *veritas transcendentalis*, transcendental not in the Kantian sense, although Kant is indeed oriented toward this concept, even if he distorts it [*verbiegt*]" (GA22: 10/8). Such distortion would entail something like an outer look, an object standing opposite a subject. But the subject–object relation for Heidegger is always grounded in a prior matrix of relationality. To pick up a hammer or pass by the field of a farmer are two examples Heidegger gives of nonobjectifying experience in *Being and Time*; to take in the redness of a rose blossom, while sitting in a garden, or to look with awe at the face of Apollo in the museum at Olympia are two examples Heidegger later gives of nonobjectifying experience of things (GA9: 73–74/58). There is no outward look, nothing standing opposite us, and yet there is the interplay of presence and absence; there is Heidegger's transcendentalism.

Why does Heidegger distance himself from his own transcendentalism in the 1930s and later? The standard answer is that it was infected with modern subjectivity. The correct answer is that it was successful in leading him beyond entities toward being and beyond the infection of modern projection toward an intensified affectivity. And as a result he could then divest himself of some of transcendental philosophy's traditional vestiges and associations.

Moving beyond Transcendental Movement

The lasting importance of transcendence in Heidegger's thought emerges clearly in the 1936 *Contributions to Philosophy*: "The *transcendental* way (but another 'transcendence') only provisionally, in order to prepare the reversing-momentum and leaping-into" (GA65: 305/215). This way alone leads us from customary, traditional ways of thinking into Heidegger's lasting topic: "When coming from the horizon of metaphysics, there is at first no other way even to make the question of being graspable as a task" (GA65: 450/317). Hence, its merit is that it makes the goal visible relative to the metaphysical focus on entities. Its demerit is twofold: It is bound to an existing tradition that obscures Heidegger's own transcendentalism; moreover, it could give the unwanted impression or illusion that the horizon stands open relative to the researcher rather than the horizon's openness being the condition for the possibility of experience. "Therefore, the effort was needed to come free of the 'condition for the possibility' as going back into the merely 'mathematical' and to grasp the truth of be-ing from within its *own* essential sway (appropriation)" (GA65: 250/176). Yet this positive reading of transcendentalism must cope with what appears to be Heidegger's unequivocal repudiation in *Contributions*:

> The "fundamental-ontological" transcendence in *Being and Time.* [a] Here the word's originary meaning is returned to it: surpassing as such; and it is grasped as the distinctive mark of human existence [*Da-sein*], in order thus to indicate that human existence [*Da-sein*] always already stands within the openness of entities. [b] This joins and, at the same time, determines more precisely "ontological" "transcendence," insofar as transcendence is grasped here in accord with human existence, i.e., originarily as *understanding of being*. [c] *But* because now understanding is also grasped as thrown projecting-open, transcendence means: standing in the truth of be-ing, indeed without initially knowing this or questioning it.
>
> [d] But now since human existence [*Da-sein*] as human existence [*Da-*sein] originarily sustains the openness of the sheltering-concealing, strictly speaking one cannot speak of a transcendence of human existence [*Da-sein*]; in the context of this approach representation of "transcendence" in *every* sense must *disappear* (GA65: 217–18/110).

What appears at first glance to be a repudiation in [d] is in fact nested in a careful set of qualifications. Heidegger does not say that his transcendentalism must be suppressed. He says that, having enacted such transcendence and arrived at its term, *then* "strictly speaking" it no longer makes sense, in *that* context, to speak of a surpassing. There is no disavowal.

In *Being and Time*, Heidegger conceives of the movement of thought from projecting being upon time to, in the final division, a turn from time to being. Hence the fundamental movement shifts from human existence's making sense of being in terms of time to time's own genesis of the various senses of being, including that of human existence itself. According to *Physics* II.1 of Aristotle, the principle that accounts for movement is the same principle that accounts for rest, for natural things move in order to rest in the achievement of their proper end. The sapling grows to achieve the form of an adult oak; the armadillo roots in order to find grub; mortals work in order that they might not be at work and enjoy leisure. The reason that Heidegger will come to say that transcendence in every sense must be suppressed is precisely because transcendence has been achieved; movement has been fulfilled. The very terminus of transcendence is immanence; we go beyond in order to tarry with whatever is our aim. "Rest is a kind of movement; only that which is able to move can rest" (GA9: 247/189).

The result is this. Heidegger makes Kant a distant prelude to *Being and Time*. Heidegger affirms that the *sui generis* transcendentalism of *Being and Time* remains the only entry way to his path of thinking. Heidegger says that, having traversed the way of *Being and Time* one then arrives at the place in which all talk of the movement of transcendence drops out, and it drops out not because it was ineffective but precisely because it was effective in leading to the lasting topic. Heidegger remains with the terminus of transcendence and hence its language of transcending must yield to a language of remaining and awaiting.

In the *Black Notebooks*, Heidegger says he fell prey to three contemporary philosophical trends. From phenomenology, he succumbed to the ideal of science, from existentialists the idea of existential modification, and from the neo-Kantians the attitude of ground-laying. (GA94: 75). The three have the effect of obscuring the crucial, underdeveloped topic, namely "the enabling of the essence" (*Ermächtigung des Wesens*) (GA94: 76, trans. modified). The contrast comes between two sorts of grounding (*Gründung*): a grounding in the experiencing of being and a grounding in thought. "The *second* beginning in its struggle with the first. The task: *on the one hand*, an original transformation of *phusis*, of *logos*, and of perception – i.e., a grounding of *alētheia*. And *on the other hand*, a dismantling of *idea* – *ousia* – the a priori and transcendence (seen on the basis of a grounding in thought)" (GA94: 213). Heidegger wishes to move from a transcendence grounded in thought to an unnamed experience of being, what I might call an affective or experiential transcendence. It does not have as its ideal the projection of being as an idea that remains statically determinative. It is not achieved by heeding the call of conscience and resolutely facing one's ownmost possibility for being. It does not occur through a process of laying the ground from thought. Instead, experience happens on the basis of experience itself withdrawing in favor of the things it enables us to experience. The failure to heed experience, then, is not the result of failing to be sufficiently scientific, existential, or critical. The failure is one that is inevitable given the nature of experience itself. To arrive at this understanding, one must first traverse *Being and Time* and in so doing "to experience in general the existence and transcendence of mankind" and then, as the title itself indicates, to move from such a unilateral to a bilateral relation to being, namely an "*enabling swing into the happening of being*" (*ermächtigendes Einschwingen in das Seinsgeschehnis*) (GA94: 57–58). Thus, "not 'transcendence' only" (GA94: 29), but transcendence plus.

Horizon and Homecoming

Kant's transcendentalism falls short of Heidegger's transcendentalism; Kant's is based in entities, Heidegger's in openness to being. Heidegger's own transcendentalism remains the way into Heidegger's one path of thinking. Its enactment reveals the limitations of its own point of departure, yet these limits can only be understood by following its course. The limitations concern the relativity of horizon to one's point of view and thus the unwanted implication that being becomes something like an object over and against this point of view Instead, being is itself a precursor to point of view; the horizon establishes the possibility of a point of view rather than vice versa. Heidegger sees this limitation as rooted in the one-sided dynamic of metaphysical language. He seeks a kind of linguisticality that is received rather than a linguisticality that is imposed. But this is clearly a modification of the transcendental, a friendly amendment as it were, rather than a new motion. Heidegger thinks the term of transcendence, when achieved, calls for the cessation of all talk of movement; hence transcendence is fulfilled in thoughts of immanence and dwelling. Heidegger's whole program, we can say, is a matter of catching up in thought to where we already are in being.

Heidegger reports that he stopped the presses on the final part of *Being and Time* because "the first form of the interpretation of being out of time leads into the *emptiness* of *thin* homeless 'conditions'" (GA82: 182, trans. Kaatz 2022a: 521). Conditions point back to an origin and horizon out toward an end but how these circumscribe a place in which to dwell remains undetermined. In this way, the fundamental critique of Heidegger's transcendentalism advanced by Edith Stein, namely, its lack of fullness (Stein 2007), was shared – at least in part – by Heidegger himself. Stein's idea, namely that one first runs one's critical or transcendental philosophy and then suspends it in view of what is revealed (2014a: 166–67), shares a certain isomorphism with Heidegger's own considered view. Transcendentalism names the attempt to catch up in thought with conditions already in play, conditions that are no mere conditions recognized by thought but instead conditions that circumscribe the place of experience quite independently of their being thought. Yet there is still more there. Experience, in the end, exceeds the scope of thought's attempt to catch up to it in terms of its timeless structures. The play of presence and absence leaves outside its scope that which presences and absences and how it presences and absences. There remains some kind of content to experience that is unable-to-be-anticipated or circumscribed by a horizon. This content, moreover, cannot therefore be separated from the transcendental framework as Heidegger shows more carefully in his meditations on the work of art and the fourfold as well as the probing reflections on the technological. This interdependence of showing and shown still falls short of the personal fullness Stein gestures toward, to be sure, but it constitutes something more than what always already circumscribes the domain of experience.[7] The house of experience, transcendentally considered, is unfurnished; the house of experience, in reality, is furnished with a contexture of things in which we discover anew the meaning of the house itself.

Did Heidegger think that the transcendentalism of *Being and Time* was problematical in virtue of its supposed subjectivity? He later comments on the sentence, "Only so long as human existence is, is there being" (SZ: 212):

> But the sentence does not mean that the human existence of the human being in the traditional sense of *existential*, and thought in modern philosophy as the actuality of the *ego cogito*, is that entity through which being is first fashioned. The sentence does not say that being is the product of the human being. The Introduction to *Being and Time* (p. 38) says simply and clearly, even in italics, "Being is the *transcendens* pure and simple." Just as the openness of spatial nearness seen from the perspective of a particular thing exceeds all things near and far, so is being essentially broader than all entities, because it is the clearing itself. For all that, being is thought on the basis of entities, a consequence of the approach – at first unavoidable – within a metaphysics that is still dominant. Only from such a perspective does being show itself in and as a transcending.
>
> The introductory definition, "Being is the *transcendens* pure and simple," articulates in one simple sentence the way the sense of being hitherto has been cleared for the human being. This retrospective definition of the essence of the being of entities from the clearing of entities as such remains indispensable for the prospective approach of thinking toward the question concerning the truth of being (GA9: 336–37/256–57).

Heidegger consistently says that transcendence is the necessary condition for accessing his lasting topic. It falls into disfavor only because it was successful in leading beyond its own resources. It is inadequate but not false, completed but not abandoned. In this way, Heidegger's critique unearths and preserves the heart of transcendentalism.

---

[7] Heidegger remains strangely and problematically indifferent to the interpersonal. "In philosophizing, *never* to think about the 'others' or about the 'thou,' but just as little about the 'I' – only about and for the origin of being. This holds equally of the matter at issue and the way [*von Sache und Weg*]." (GA94: 28). On the interconnection of being and the person, see, among other things, Engelland (2004) and Engelland (2010).

2 The Metaphysics of Transcendence

The Kant interpretation of the years 1925 through early 1928, marked by an intellectual conversion and culminating in a four-hour lecture course, differs from the interpretation of 1928 and 1929, which takes Kant as a "refuge" and issues in the only complete monograph Heidegger ever published, *Kant and the Problem of Metaphysics*. For, when we compare the sprawling four-hour 1927–28 lecture course (GA25) with the compact 1929 Kant book (GA3), we find that the latter is not a digest of the former. In both texts, it is true, Heidegger presents a phenomenological Kant who subordinates thought to intuition and who labors to unearth the spring of experience itself. But in the lecture course there is no mention of the inner architectonic of the *Critique of Pure Reason*, an inner architectonic that diverges from the explicit structure of the work, even though in the Kant book it becomes a central concern. What is at work in the inner architectonic? Here reading the text in light of the 1928 lecture course on Leibniz (GA26) is eye-opening. Heidegger retraces Leibniz's metaphysical critique of clarity and distinctness as sufficient criteria for grasping truth, because they fail to show the inner harmony necessary for all real possibility. The Kant book is the Kant book because Heidegger works to show that Kant, for a moment, displays the real possibility of experience in terms of the inner architectonic of the work. The preponderance of the term "metaphysics" in the Kant book and the absence of the term in the earlier interpretation reflects this difference. There is indeed an identifiable shift between two phases of Heidegger's enthusiastic reading of Kant: the pre-Leibnizian Husserlian phase and the post-Leibnizian metaphysical phase.

This section details Heidegger's brilliant but brief syncretistic union of the transcendental philosophy of Aristotle and of Kant. The leading idea of this synthesis is that both ancient and modern philosophy focus on the openness of the human to being. The ancient, however, also pursues essential metaphysical questions of the a priori perfect form: what it was to be. Heidegger turns to Kant to advance an anti-neo-Kantian reading of Kant in which Kant appears as a more sophisticated follower of the ancients, whose project of inquiring into the condition for the possibility of experience is in fact a metaphysics (or analytic) of the essence of transcendence. The critical distance of the later period will take issue with just this metaphysics of projective unveiling, not the prior transcendence of affective experience.

Evidence of a Shift

In 1973, Heidegger penned an introduction to the fourth edition of the Kant book. He retracts the book as an interpretation of Kant but not as an introduction to the horizon of questioning operative in *Being and Time* (GA3: xiv–xv).[8] For our purposes, what is decisive is the claim that the Kant book departs from the interpretation mapped out in *Being and Time* just insofar as it offers a "progressive" interpretation. Does the late Heidegger remember correctly that his relation to Kant shifts between *Being and Time*, written in 1926, and the Kant book of 1929? Heidegger even again points to the 1927–28 lecture course, as he had done in the preface to the first edition, and identifies it as the place where the transformation takes place, and he even points to the schematism as the decisive issue.

Now, Heidegger does clearly misremember the issue: It was not the schematism but the question of the metaphysics of transcendence that marked the innovation, since the schematism had already attracted his notice two years earlier. Yet Heidegger is right that the reading of Kant in the published *Being and Time* differs from the reading of Kant in the Kant book. There is only a phenomenology of transcendence in *Being and Time* but in what Kisiel (1993: 451) terms the "publication blitz" of 1929 there is something more: a metaphysics of transcendence. This innovation stems indeed from the 1927–28 lecture course in which he writes, "Transcendental possibility refers to the factual content of a subject matter, determines it in *what* it is, and thus circumscribes what this matter must be in order to get realized as this what. Therefore, in Kant *transcendental* possibility is the *real* possibility as distinguished from logical possibility" (GA25: 187). It was the 1928 lecture course on Leibniz which was decisive for the new interpretation and sets the stage for the Kant book in which Heidegger sought to find in the inner architectonic of the *Critique of Pure Reason* the real essence of transcendence. It may have been the case that the essentials of the Kant book could be found in the 1927–28 lecture course but it was only in the 1928 course in which the strategy emerged for forging these various essentials into one adequate essence. In place of *Being and Time*'s affective-resolute unveiling of the ecstatic horizon of temporality we have the projective ground-laying of the essence of transcendence.

It is crucial to register this shift, because then one can clearly see that the later rejection of the metaphysics of transcendence does not entail a rejection of the prior phenomenology of transcendence. To question the adequacy of the Kant

[8] Morganna Lambeth (2023) approaches the Kant book as an exercise in hermeneutical charity in which Heidegger avoids the dangers of maximizing agreement at the expense of otherness ("ventriloquism"). In this way, we do not just learn something about Heidegger but also Kant in the exchange. My own view is that Heidegger was right to think that the Kant book fell prey to ventriloquism in its horizon of questioning, but that the new interpretation, which he offers as a supplement, corrects it in a manner that is also quite charitable and productive (Engelland 2017). In any event, it is Heidegger's transcendentalism rather than the merits or demerits of Heidegger's changing interpretations of Kant's transcendentalism that is our concern at present.

book and its metaphysics of transcendence does not undermine the phenomenological transcendentalism of *Being and Time* in which projection is counterpoised to thrownness, existentiality to facticity. Only in the metaphysics of transcendence, in the problem of the ground-laying, does projection come to the center and does the historicity of affectivity effectively drop out. The later shift from the metaphysics of transcendence is in many ways a return to transcendental phenomenology, the affective transcendentalism, first worked out in *Being and Time* in terms of thrown projection. Philosophy begins in wonderment, not ground laying, and Heidegger will come to see that its renewal comes through a rekindled and deepened wonderment (Engelland 2017: 188–94).

The Metaphysics of Essence

In 1926, Heidegger credits Leibniz for the decisive and positive modern innovation. "Up to Leibniz, the problem of foundation remained unclarified; foundation and cause were not distinguished. It was thus among the Greeks and in scholasticism" (GA22: 225/179). It is this distinction that explains Heidegger's program of fundamental ontology in *Being and Time*. That is, there is no ontotheological inquiry into causality but instead a phenomenological exhibition of the foundation for making sense of being. Yet such fundamental ontology is not yet a metaphysics of transcendence.

In the 1928 lecture course on Leibniz, Heidegger develops the full significance of this distinction between foundation and cause by helping himself to more of the Leibnizian program: Heidegger sees in Leibniz's critique of Descartes's criteria of clarity and distinctness a decisive development in the understanding of essence. For it is not enough for an essence merely to be clearly and distinctly grasped in its noncontradictoriness; it is necessary, further, that it be grasped in its inner unifying compatibility. An essence is not a juxtaposition; an essence is internally united. "Adequate knowledge as knowledge of essence is a priori knowledge of what makes the known itself possible, for it is the clear grasp of thorough compatibility, *compatibilitas*" (GA26: 80). Heidegger painstakingly maps the contours of the Leibnizian doctrine of essence, and he does so to counter the neo-Kantian epistemological or Cartesian reading of Kant, because Kant too distinguishes real and nominal definition on this Leibnizian basis.

Heidegger does note that the Leibnizian monadology was really an account of entities rather than an account of the openness of a particular entity, human existence, toward all other things in light of being. Hence he must subject the monad to reconstructive surgery (GA26: 270–71). Leibniz had all the resources he needed to offer a metaphysical or foundational (rather than causal) account of human existence. But he did not complete the project. For that, we need Kant's *Critique of Pure Reason* as a fulfilment of the metaphysics of transcendence.

Again, a curious, but often overlooked feature of the 1929 Kant book is its obsession with the *Critique of Pure Reason*'s inner architectonic (GA3: 43). And it is overlooked precisely because the Kant book is not read in tandem with the Leibniz lecture course and the idea of adequation. For Heidegger says there that the Leibnizian distinction between epistemological clarification and metaphysical adequacy is central to his anti-neo-Kantian reading of Kant (GA26: 81). The epistemological framework of attaining clarity and distinctness establishes only a nominal definition and fails to achieve the higher metaphysical unveiling of essence, which is accomplished by means of grasping and exhibiting the inner harmony of the reality in question. "Leibniz provides not only more rigorous concepts of clarity and obscurity, distinctness and confusion, but he shows there is an essentially higher stage above them, where we first attain knowledge of essence, since here the totality of the necessary marks of realities are first revealed" (GA26: 82). The focus on clarity and distinctness is superseded by the question of adequacy and this in turn is ordered to appropriation: "Those mentioned earlier (*obscura–clara, confusa–distincta, inadaequata–adaequata*) each refers to a stage of analysis, a step in making explicit marks and moments of marks (*requisita*). With the last distinction, however, we are dealing with a possible double way of appropriating [*Aneignen*] and possessing the adequate, the completely analyzed as such" (GA26: 78). Yet Heidegger is clear that Leibniz merely prepares for what Kant alone achieves. "Leibniz's thought is only a preparation for the eventual separation of metaphysical from non-metaphysical knowledge. The separation emerges with Kant, and then it is again completely buried" (GA26: 89). In the Kant book, Heidegger advances a metaphysical interpretation of the text as focused exclusively on the question of the essence or possibility of transcendence in terms of the ultimate source of experience. Ground-laying, he writes, is "the architectonic circumscription and delineation of the inner possibility of metaphysics, that is, the concrete determination of its essence. All determination of essence, however, is first achieved in the setting-free [*Freilegung*] of the essential ground" (GA3: 2). See Table 3.

The essence of transcendence is freedom, a freedom expressed in Leibniz's principle of sufficient reason and its ultimate question: Why is there something rather than nothing? In the "rather than," Heidegger says there is a reference to transcendental freedom: "For this *potius* is only the expression of the surpassingness of world, of the upswing of freedom into possibility" (GA26: 384). Yet this transcendence is not affective or responsive; it is based on the modern *conatus* or drive rather than the medieval understanding of power as receptivity. Heidegger's metaphysics of transcendence, loosely inspired by Leibniz and

Table 3 The five stages of the ground-laying

	Kant and the Problem of Metaphysics	**The corresponding Leibnizian stages**
1	essential elements of pure knowledge: intuition and thought	(a) clear (versus obscure) and (b) distinct (versus confused)
2	essential unity of pure knowledge in the transcendental imagination	
3	inner possibility of ontological synthesis in the transcendental deduction	(c) adequate (versus inadequate)
4	the ground of the inner possibility of ontological knowledge in terms of the temporal schematism	
5	the essence of transcendence in the highest principle of all synthetic judgments	(d) intuitive (versus symbolic)

Kant, manifests a peculiarly modern voluntarism. That is, it is correlated with an existential moment of willing to catch up in thought to being through the adequate unveiling of transcendence: "The metaphysics of human existence, which is to be cultivated in Fundamental Ontology, is not claimed to be a new discipline within the framework of these which are already at hand. Rather, in it is demonstrated the will to the awakening of the insight that philosophizing occurs as the explicit transcendence of human existence" (GA3: 242). We have here, in the projective unveiling of transcendence, the willing to have a horizon, which was flagged in the last section as the genuine shortcoming of the transcendental approach. Yet in the 1929–30 lecture course (GA29/30), which he says is a new beginning, the ground-laying falls out and fundamental moods return from their marginalization. The metaphysics of transcendence gives way to an exuberance of affectivity, with fundamental moods, such as wonder and terror, again becoming central, together with a language evocative of and responsive to this experience. By the time of the *Contributions* (GA65), Heidegger has a full-blown affective transcendentalism in play.

After scrapping his first draft of SZ I.3, he turned to metaphysics but to no avail. "The division in question was held back because thinking failed in the adequate saying of this turning [*Kehre*] and did not succeed with the help of the language of metaphysics" (GA9: 328/250). The help of metaphysics refers to the help of Leibniz, whom, he says in 1928, enabled him to go beyond the inquiry of transcendence developed in *Being and Time* (GA26: 245). Yet the metaphysical beyond constituted a transgression; it amounted to a betrayal of the subject matter.

What needed to be retained, then, was a phenomenology no longer conceived in terms of a research program into the scientific domain of the a priori.

> In the poverty of its first breakthrough, the thinking that tries to advance thought into the truth of being brings only a small part of that wholly other dimension to language. This language even falsifies itself for it does not yet succeed in retaining the essential help of phenomenological seeing while dispensing with the inappropriate concern with "science" and "research" (GA9: 357/271).

The metaphysics of transcendence was a brief but fascinating moment of Heidegger's transcendentalism, but he rejects it as being based on projection and hence subjectivity rather than phenomenological disclosure. Yet it has the following value as a hypothetical: Supposing one wanted to unveil the site of Heidegger's topic using the resources of the modern metaphysical tradition, what would that look like? And the answer is that it would not be based on clear and distinct perception alone but instead on appropriating the adequate comprehension of the inner unity of the whole ground circumscribed by temporal horizons. See Table 4.

Transcendence in History

Heidegger thinks the metaphysics of transcendence fails, because it falls prey to two prejudices: the ancient logical prejudice which interprets being in terms of entities and the modern version of this prejudice that does so in terms of the entity par excellence, the human subject. First, the metaphysics of transcendence falls prey to the *logical prejudice* (Dahlstrom 2001). Heidegger comes to think that there is no such thing as a *metaphysics* of transcendence, for the simple reason that metaphysics always interprets being in relation to entities and never the movement of experience as such. In 1930, in the context of exploring Kant's metaphysics of causality, Heidegger writes:

Table 4 Three ways of expressing the phenomenology of transcendence

Year	Representative text	Language	Elucidation
1927	*Being and Time* (SZ)	existential	affective and authentic disclosure of experience
1929	*Kant and the Problem of Metaphysics* (GA3)	metaphysical	authentic projection of the complete essence of experience
1936	*Contributions* (GA65)	poetical/ rhetorical	affective and historical disclosure of experience

> The "and" is the actual crux of the problem. The leading questions – what are entities? – must itself be transformed into the fundamental question, i.e. into the question which inquires into the "and" of being and time and thus into the ground *of both*. This fundamental question is: *what is the essence of time, such that it grounds being, and such that the question of being as the leading question of metaphysics can and must be unfolded within this horizon*? (GA31: 116/82).

The metaphysics of transcendence fails due to the limited horizon of metaphysics, but it fails, therefore, just insofar as it fails to catch up, conceptually, to the phenomenology of transcendence. Heidegger's transcendence squared exceeds Kant's version of transcendence, which remains within the horizon of metaphysics. Second, it falls prey to the *mathematical prejudice* (Engelland 2017), that peculiar modern permutation of the logical prejudice, according to which the human subject becomes the ground of our knowledge of objects by means of projecting objectivity. To be sure, at no point does Heidegger himself identify transcendence with metaphysics in the narrow sense of the logical prejudice, nor does he identify it with subjectivity in the narrow sense of the mathematical prejudice, but instead he comes to see that his charitable, that is, violent reading of the tradition, obscured rather than illumined the path for others to follow.

The fundamental critique of the metaphysics of transcendence comes in the 1935–36 lecture course, *The Question Concerning the Thing*, in which it is argued that transcendental ground-laying constitutes an extreme version of the modern mathematical prejudice, which deploys a projection rooted in a subject, itself a ramification of the ancient logical prejudice, which has eyes for entities alone; what both miss is the presubjective and preobjective horizon of world. Yet Heidegger argues that it is precisely the transcendental turn of Kant, as reflected in the projection of the *Critique of Pure Reason*, that opens the possibility of overcoming both the modern mathematical prejudice and the ancient logical prejudice; the focus on *pure* reason, rooted in the affectivity of intuition, undermines the hold of the mathematical, and the focus on pure *reason*, rooted in the interplay of self and other, brings to light the pretheoretical context in which we encounter things, thereby undermining the ancient logical prejudice (GA41: 123). At the heart of Kant's transcendentalism is the between, which leads beyond the metaphysics of things and the metaphysics of subjectivity to Heidegger's phenomenon of transcendence (GA41: 244–45. As Kisiel observes,

> Kant's transcendental reflection, which first found its locus in the movement of thought to its object, now finds itself drawn into a movement of reciprocal grounding between the subjectivity of the subject and the objectivity of the

> object, where the 'between' suggests the ground of a more original unity as the essence of transcendence (experience). Going *back* to this ground would then be a more basic transcendental reflection, one which Heidegger assumes as his own task (1973:113).

Kant's transcendentalism at once marks the culmination of modern thought and the threshold for a new beginning; that is, historically considered, it is Kant's projective transcendentalism that, despite its great distance, comes nearest and closest to Heidegger's affective transcendentalism.

In sum, the peculiar hybrid, a metaphysics of transcendence, which cannot be identified with either the ancients or the moderns, but is an innovation of Heidegger's, is rejected because it was at once too modern and too ancient. Its focus on ground-laying was a projection, rooted in the mathematical prejudice, itself rooted in the logical prejudice. Yet it was an attempted advance on the transcendence of *Being and Time*; its retraction leaves Heidegger's phenomenology intact, at the very moment in which it reaches beyond its own native resources to articulate the ultimate contexture of experience.

3 The Phenomenology of Transcendence

It may seem as though transcendence has little to do with being, but it is precisely the question of being that leads Heidegger to explore the movement of transcendence. Being's ontological transcending of entities mirrors experience's timely transcending of things. Heidegger's hunch is that ontological transcendence has the same basis that supports experiential transcendence. Being and time are interwoven.

Heidegger, we know, becomes increasingly critical of his transcendentalism and even comes to censure his novel metaphysics of transcendence, which he worked out on the basis of certain passages from Leibniz and Kant, but he retains the intrinsic interconnection of being and experience. In this way, he not only appropriates the horizon of transcendental thought; he endeavors to deepen it by working out a more fundamental level of transcendental reciprocity in terms of being and time. While among the ancients, Aristotle clarifies the many senses of being in terms of their relatedness to substance, and, among the moderns, Kant clarifies experience in terms of the unifying power of the transcendental imagination, and, among contemporary authors, Husserl clarifies intelligibility in terms of the synthesis of inner time consciousness, Heidegger wishes to clarify the many senses of being in terms of their relatedness to time's unifying ecstatic-horizonal dynamism. He even speaks occasionally of a kind of transcendental science of the horizon of temporality, and he experiments regularly with a transcendental vocabulary of Latinate terms, such as *presence*, signalling his wish to develop the transcendental tradition.

The Meaning of Being

Philosophy is not a positive science, because its topic, the transcendence of being, is hidden and must first be uncovered before it can be explicated (GA22: 10–11). The Middle Ages coined the word transcendentals "because these determinations lie *beyond* each concrete determinacy of being [*Seinsbestimmtheit*] and, for their part, determine each being [*Sein*]" (GA17: 177). To philosophize, then, means in the first place to catch up to hidden being by going beyond entities.

In *De veritate*, Thomas sketches a return that constitutes the life of an intellectual being (Aquinas 1952: q. 1, a. 9). Instead of being simply and straightforwardly directed to a *res*, the soul reflects, turning its attention first to the act by which it is directed to the *res*, then to the power of the act grounded in the nature of the intellect itself (GA17: 179–80). Here in this neo-Platonic triple is the schema of the first division of *Being and Time*: first, a kind of engrossed being directed toward things (SZ 1.1); second, a return to one's own agency in authenticity (SZ 1.2); third, an elucidation of the nature of the understanding itself (SZ 1.3). In place of reflection, Heidegger will deploy resolution, and in place of nature as the ultimate explanation, Heidegger will place time. Yet the very sense of a return unmistakably carries over. As Heidegger glosses Thomas in a lecture course leading up to *Being and Time*: "This *reditio completa* constitutes the perfection of this being [*Sein*] insofar as, through this reditio, every entity that is grasped by the intellectus is also taken up and appropriated [*angeeignet*]. Through being-able-to-take-up in this manner what is known and grasped, this entity itself increases in *amplitudo*, in the scope of being [*Sein*]" (GA17: 181). This return brings out the very being of the understanding in its fundamental openness to the being of things.

> The character of the soul is not taken as a transition, an historical occurrence, in the sense that the soul goes out to some entity. Instead, *being-directed-at a res* [*das* Entgegengerichtetsein *auf* res] pertains to the nature of the intellectus. This openness for the entity [*Diese Aufgeschlossenheit für das Seiende*] is not something imported, but instead pertains, along with other things, to the being of the intellectus itself (GA17: 179).

Despite this kinship with the transcendental philosophy of the ancients, Heidegger thinks that in light of creation and the fact that both the human soul and the related *res* are created by God, the mysterious character of truth is hidden for Thomas behind a simple relation of one created being to another (GA17: 183–87). In this way, Heidegger regards Thomas in unnecessarily simplistic terms (McGrath 2006). Among other things, Heidegger overlooks the fundamental significance of *aliquid* in Thomas's thought, for to be "something" belongs to a matrix of intelligibility that we in our intellectual openness can experience and understand (Aquinas 1952: q. 1, a. 1; Rosemann 1996).

Heidegger's transcendentalism takes its justification from the very transcendence of being. Yet, having gone beyond entities, Heidegger now wishes us to go beyond being in order to reveal the ultimate horizon for making sense of being and hence the being of things. He finds this in the transcendental horizon of time. As being transcends entities, so time transcends being. Human existence, in light of understanding being, can transcend entities, and it can do so, ultimately, thanks to temporality. Time is the condition for the possibility of experiencing the being of things.

Human existence ranges out beyond things and thereby encounters them in their otherness. What enables this transcendence is the ecstatic-horizon movement of original time, which opens up various avenues of development. Hence, Heidegger does not wonder about entities; he wonders about the being of entities, and he does so in terms of time. In doing so, he thinks he is redirecting the traditional horizon of metaphysical questioning. In 1930, he writes,

> The 'and' is the actual crux of the problem. The leading question – what are entities? – must itself be transformed into the fundamental question, i.e. into the question which inquires into the 'and' of being and time and thus into the ground *of both*. This fundamental question is: *what is the essence of time, such that it grounds being, and such that the question of being as the leading question of metaphysics can and must be unfolded within this horizon*? (GA31, 116/82).

Throughout the 1930s, he does not fail to repeat that while the tradition remains anchored in entities, he himself ventures out into the pre-entitative horizon. Even if he becomes hesitant about the terminology of the horizon, with its possible illusion of standing opposite the subject rather than conditioning subjectivity, what the term names, the limit of experience, remains in play. Emphasizing the genuine facticity of transcendental philosophy (Kraatz 2022b), which is present in Heidegger's transcendentalism from the start, is key to working against the illusion that the horizon stands open only relative to the gaze of the researcher.

Transcendence, as a stepping beyond, is accomplished in timeliness's ecstatic and horizonal character. Each of the three ecstases of time carry us beyond ourselves, but the carrying beyond is also determined by limits or horizons. It is this ecstatic-horizonal structured movement that gives rise to world as the place of experience. Temporally expressed, the stepping of transcendence is "ecstatic," and the term of the stepping is "horizon": "Ecstases are not simply raptures in which one gets carried away. Rather, there belongs to each ecstasis a 'whereto' of getting carried away. This 'whereto' of the ecstasis we call the 'horizonal schema'" (SZ: 365; see also GA24: 429). The temporal genesis of world comes from time's ecstatic and horizonal character. Heidegger thinks that the transcendencies or series of goings beyond rebound at the horizons that determine the ecstases constituting originative temporality.

> Because the ecstatic-horizonal unity of timeliness is intrinsically self-projection pure and simple, because as ecstatic it makes possible all projecting upon ... and represents, together with the horizon belonging to the ecstasis, the condition of possibility of an toward-which, an out-toward-which in general, it can no longer be asked upon what the schemata can on their part be projected, and so on in infinitum. The series, mentioned earlier, of projections as it were inserted one before the other – understanding of entities, projection upon being, understanding of being, projection upon time – has its end at the horizon of ecstatic unity of timeliness. ... But this end is nothing but the beginning and starting point for the possibility of all projecting (GA24: 437).

Thus Heidegger sees the horizon as at once the end of and the origin of the dynamism of experience. The temporal terminus of transcendence is the same as the temporal origination of transcendence.

Consider the ecstatic-horizonal character of a particular experience such as surfing. Out beyond the breaking waves, I sit atop my board, scanning the visual horizon for the first signs of the swell-to-come. While waiting, I might run my hand over the wax smeared on the board, I might notice the keen bite of the sea's cold on my bare skin, or I might ward off light from the glaring sun. But all such entities lapse into absence when I see that the wave approaches. Paddling hard, I strain with the hope that I might join my momentum to the wave's sheer power. If I am successful, I pay no heed to the wax, the water, or the sun, but instead focus solely on the way the flexing of my limbs allows me to ease ever down and into the wave's raw, unfolding power.

What Heidegger wants us to catch sight of, in his transcendental analysis of this or any other experience, is the fact that the continual shift from some present item to another happens thanks to the unfolding of temporality and its interplay of presence and absence. After all, we speak of making an entity present when we focus on it. The wax of the board, for example, is there in its application as something handy for gripping and thus for surfing; the wax is there in its use as something inconspicuous – unless it fails. If it does, I will turn explicitly toward it:

"Why did I slip off the board? I must have accidently used warm water wax instead of cold water wax, so that it hardened too much." Heidegger says that the shift from that which is unthematic to thematic, from handy to on-hand, is a shift in being which has a temporal basis. That is, we understand an entity in terms of being, whether handy or on-hand, but we understand handy or on-hand, in turn, in terms of the modalization of temporality. Heidegger names the peculiar play of presence and absence *praesens*. "The handiness of the handy, the being of these entities, is understood as praesens, a praesens which, as non-conceptually understandable, is already unveiled in the self-projection of timeliness, by means of whose bringing forth anything like existent commerce with entities handy and on-hand becomes possible" (GA24: 438–39, translation modified). *Praesens*, then, constitutes that aspect of the self-explication of time that enables the understanding of entities. We do not project the horizon; time itself, in its unfolding, opens up this possibility for our understanding. Time, not human subjectivity, enables me to attend to the inconspicuous handiness of the wax or its conspicuous on-handness: Both have their own temporal profile, their own peculiar experiential complex.

SZ 1.1 moves beyond entities to being; SZ 1.2 moves beyond being to timeliness: SZ 1.3 makes the turn – it rebounds – by moving back from temporality as the ultimate horizon of understanding to being; it accomplished the turn from the projection of being upon time to the advent of being from time.

> Thus the significance-relationships which determine the structure of the world are not a network of forms which a wordless subject has laid over some kind of material. What is rather the case is that factical human existence, understanding itself and its world ecstatically in the unity of the "there", comes back from these horizons to the entities encountered within them (SZ: 396).

The projection, in other words, merely tried to catch up to its prior possibility. Time qua horizon of being is temporality or the transcendental horizon.

> Transcendence first of all makes possible existence in the sense of comporting oneself to oneself as an entity, to others as entities, and to entities in the sense of either the handy or the on-hand. Thus transcendence as such, in the sense of our interpretation, is the first condition of possibility of the understanding of being, the first and nearest upon which an ontology has to project being . . . . The science of being thus constituted we call the science that inquires and interprets in the light of transcendence properly understood: *transcendental science* (GA24: 460).

At the heart of Heidegger's analysis is the fact that time itself constitutes the primal movement of experience which throws open the various possibilities in which we can make sense of things. It is time, not human existence, that enables human existence. It is time, not human existence, that enables the focal point

Table 5 Heidegger on transcendence

	Text	Topic	Horizon of questioning	Answer
T[1]	SZ 1.1–2	the correlation of language and thing in terms of the between	How must we be to access things in their independence?	cast open ecstatically and horizonally
T[2]	SZ 1.3	the correlation of language and being in terms of (a) projecting a horizon and (b) affective openness	How does the interplay of presence and absence let being be?	by casting open various complexes appropriate to the different kinds of things

and halo of experience. By entering into this happening, the unfolding of time, we become what we are, those that can experience the being of things. Heidegger's transcendental science is the science of the possibility of experience in terms of the phenomenological interplay of presence and absence (Engelland 2020a). See Table 5.

Veritas Transcendentalis and the Truth of Being

In the ambit of *Being and Time*, Heidegger envisions a genuine science of being based in transcendental truth. Such a science is a critical science in contrast to positive science. The subject matter of the critical science is not pre-given or available in a straightforward natural experience as are the objects of all the other science; instead, its subject matter is naturally hidden and can be discovered only through an act of differentiation. Hence Heidegger's sought science is unlike any other in being critical, based on an explicit act of *critein* that unearths its subject matter through differentiating entities and their being (GA22: 7–11). Nonetheless, Heidegger does not shy away from characterizing it as a genuine science just insofar as it subordinates itself to the subject matter by having it stand before us, a process he terms "objectification": ". . . *timeliness* is *the root* and the *ground for* both *the possibility* and, properly understood, the *factical necessity of the objectification of the given entities and the given being*" (GA24: 456). Phenomenology is the temporal science, because it provides the horizon for making sense of being. It traces all back to temporal projection (*not* timely projection, i.e., *not* the projection of human existence, but instead the self-explication of temporality thanks to which all the projections of human existence are possible). Heidegger's objectification of being, then, is the inverse of all other scientific projections, which make an object stand over and against a subject. Instead, understood from out of the turn intrinsic to the program outlined for SZ 1.3, it is the very logic of temporality that gives rise to understanding. "Because temporal projection makes possible an objectification of being and assures conceptualizability, and thereby constitutes ontology in general as a science, we call this science in distinction from the positive sciences the *temporal science*" (GA24: 459–60). Heidegger thinks temporal projection accomplishes two aims: It presents being as such, and it makes being as such intelligible.

Regarding conceptualizability: Heidegger tells us that the transcendental science is expressed using a particular grammatical tense he terms, variously, the "a priori perfect," "ontological," or "transcendental" tense (SZ: 114). The idea, which Heidegger notes finds expression in both Latin and Greek, is that we understand the condition for the possibility of something by coming back to that which is, in an original sense, prior. Heidegger sees this at work in the way Aristotle discusses essence and Kant the schematism. He thinks he is uniting the best of the moderns and the ancients with the help of the conceptuality furnished by the Latin language. The a priori perfect names the earlier that enables; it articulates the originative character of temporality. "*Time is earlier than any possible earlier* of whatever sort, because it is the basic condition for an earlier as such. And because time as the source of all enablings (possibilities) is the earliest, all possibilities as such in their possibility-making function have the character of the earlier. That is to say, they are a priori" (GA24: 463).

Regarding objectification: Heidegger's later thinking will realize the infelicity of the term "objectivity" and its attendant conceptualization. Objectivization involves two challenges. First, it gives rise to the illusion that being is an object opposite the human subject, but at no point does Heidegger ever maintain this thesis. Second, it succumbs to the analogy that as subject is to object so time is to being. But the relation of time to being is not the relation of a subject to an object. There is nothing entitative about time and nothing object-like about the senses of being that it engenders. Hence phenomenology needs to avail itself of other language.

Yet we do find something strangely un-Heideggerian lurking in the pages of *Being and Time*. The hiddenness of being cannot be cancelled so that being is made present; being cannot be, as Heidegger puts it in startling Baconian terms in *Being and Time*, "wrested" (SZ: 36, 222, 311, 313; see Sheehan 2015b: 220–21). It is not being in terms of time that must stand before us but it is we who must bring ourselves to a stand before being and time. We must subordinate ourselves to its natural, historical rhythm rather than impose one of our own in the fashion of every modern *mathesis universalis*. Truth is not a function of authenticity but of being appropriated. As Heidegger carefully put it in notes for the 1937–38 lecture course: "Being [*das Seyn*] is not merely hidden; it withdraws and conceals itself. From this we derive an essential insight: the clearing [*die Lichtung*], in which entities are, is not simply bounded and delimited by something hidden but by something self-concealing [*Sichverbergendes*]" (GA45: 210).

Hiddenness corresponds to research, but the condition for the possibility of experience is not hidden in virtue of not being sought; it is hidden in virtue of being the origin of experience and so necessarily occluded by the very experienced things it enables us to meet with. Thought from the ground up, the ground as it were withdraws; the backgrounding of the background is what enables the foregrounding of the foreground. Hence, the issue which provokes Heidegger's critical distance to his erstwhile transcendentalism is not principally the impossibility of arriving at the ultimate source of experience. It is simply this: The transcendence of human existence, operating in the modality of inauthentic absorption and authentic research, reveals the clearing by way of a glance that lacks depth. The transcendental movement of human experience yields to the depth dimension of "time as the transcendental horizon," which he later glosses as the truth of being. It is thus not Heidegger's worry that transcendentalism is circular or begs the question by presupposing the ground it seeks to disclose (Sheehan 2015b: 227–28). It is rather the great merit of transcendentalism to implicate the naturally hidden origin by means of its circular back and forth relatedness, undercutting at once the modern mathematical prejudice as well as the ancient logical one (Engelland 2017: 123–57).

Despite this important reservation and shift in emphasis, the very relation between inquiry and subject matter, developed so expertly in terms of transcendence, persists as the emphasis shifts from the activity of the researcher to the receptivity of the one claimed by being. Hence, Heidegger moves toward a presubjective affective transcendentalism (Engelland 2017: 170–98). "This reciprocity of *needing* and *belonging* makes up be-ing as appropriation; and the first thing that is incumbent upon thinking is to raise the swinging of this reciprocity [*die Schwingung dieses Gegenschwunges*] into the simplicity of knowledge and to ground the reciprocity in its truth" (GA65: 251). Transcendence ventures forth unilaterally. This unilateral movement is not annulled. Rather, it is taken up into a more comprehensive bilateral movement. The centrality of the heart, which in *Being and Time* Heidegger appropriates from the Augustinian tradition, reemerges after the modern metaphysical language of ground-laying proves inadequate to bring transcendence to its proper fulfilment. The heart and its fundamental affectivity constitutes the most profound development of Heidegger's phenomenological transcendentalism (Wood 2015b; Wood 2018).

4 The Transcendence of Things

Heidegger's transcendentalism begins and ends by taking for granted that things are and can be manifest to us as they are. Heidegger's transcendental question concerns the nature of our openness that affords the possibility for such manifestation. "How must the finite entity that we call 'human' be according to its innermost essence so that it can be at all open to an entity that it itself is not and that therefore must be able to show itself from itself?" (GA3: 43). Openness to otherness is at the heart of the transcendental movement of SZ 1.1–2. And it leads to the ultimate concern of SZ 1.3 only in such a way that entities retain their original independence. "From whence are we at all to comprehend the like of being, with the entire wealth of articulations and references which are included in it?" (GA3: 224).[9] Hence a certain Heideggerian realism or transcendence of things is the necessary condition for Heideggerian transcendentalism to get off the ground.[10]

Heidegger, like Thomas, defines truth in terms of the openness of understanding to things; hence, without such openness, things can no longer be said to be true (SZ: 14, 227). Does this succumb to relativism? Thomas can say that absent such openness things might not be true but they nonetheless remain real in the strict sense that they have their own native intelligibility (*res*). Heidegger, without having recourse to the language of *res*, has to say something similar lest openness become conflated with projection, and he says the content of expressions subsists independently of us (GA24: 315). Indeed it is significant, in this regard, that in the mid-1930s he begins to ask earnestly what is a *thing*, the traditional translation of the Latin *res*.

How does this thingly subsistence interface with manifestation? Heidegger does not quite ask that. Instead he asks only how we can be so that things can be manifest to us as they are. That is, he does not turn his philosophical energies to the question of subsistence per se. Instead, presupposing such subsistence as a given, he turns to how we can *access* it without confecting it.

> 1) Entities are in themselves the kinds of entities they are, and in the way they are, even if, for example, human existence does not exist. 2) Being "is" not, but being is there [*es gibt*], insofar as human existence exists. In the essence of existence there is transcendence, i.e., a giving of world prior to and for all

[9] Heidegger italicizes this question.

[10] On Heidegger's realism about entities, see Carman 2003: 155–203; Engelland 2017: 224–27; Engelland 2020a: 201–02; Kinkaid 2019.

> being-toward-and-among intra-worldly entities. 3) Only insofar as existing human existence gives itself anything like being can entities emerge in their in-themselves, i.e., can the first claim likewise be understood at all and be taken into account (GA26: 194–195).

With the question of access, I do not mean to suggest that Heidegger is taking the transcendental question in a modern manner as the question about how a subject, for the most part enclosed within its own subjective sphere, can "go out to" an object other than it. Rather this version of the question becomes repurposed and superseded by the question of how human existence, dwelling with others in the shared world, can make sense of the being of things. The question concerns the conditions under which being and things are made available to us for understanding: ". . . *timeliness* is *the root* and the *ground for* both *the possibility* and, properly understood, the *factical necessity of the objectification of the given entities and the given being*" (GA24: 456). The recessive unfolding of timeliness as temporality enables the accessing of entities; presencing simultaneously makes something present *and* occludes itself, and it actually makes something present by means of this very self-occlusion. Something is foregrounded only by virtue of the backgrounding of the background.

Realism and the Question of Relativism

How can Heidegger be a realist when he is regularly accused of idealism? Here I will argue that if John Searle, a fierce critic of Heidegger's supposed idealism, is a realist, then so is Heidegger – and a more effective one at that. For both Searle and Heidegger espouse what we could call "pretheoretical metaphysical realism." They both rightly insist that, independent of our theories about it and as a condition for the possibility of our theories, there is a way the world is. In formulating realism, they do not dogmatically assert that the world is this way or that, but only that there is a way that it is. All our theories, however true they may prove to be, presuppose this pretheoretical ground. Searle begins the definition of realism as follows: "*Realism is the view that there is a way that things are that is logically independent of all human representations*" (1995: 155). The important qualifier is the word, "logically." If it were absent, the definition would be indistinguishable from skepticism even if mitigated in the form of Kant's thing-in-itself. That is, the skeptic would likely agree that "there is a way that things are that is independent of all human representations." What distinguishes realism from skepticism is not the independence of things *simpliciter*, but our ability to access them in their independence. Accordingly, Searle inserts "logically" to mean that we can in fact represent the way things are in such a way that this representing does not compromise the independence of things.

Searle finishes the definition of realism by categorically excluding any particular theories about what there is: "*Realism does not say how things are but only that there is a way that they are*" (1995: 155). He amplifies the pre-theoretical character of realism with this qualification, "And 'things' in the previous two sentences does not mean material objects or even objects. It is, like the 'it' in 'It is raining,' not a referring expression" (1995: 155). In the definition, then, Searle deliberately distinguishes realism from any theories about the way things are. Realism is a pretheoretical claim, because it is a condition for there to be theories at all, whether these be scientific theories about neuroscience, however grounded, or everyday theories about child-rearing. Realism is not committed, as Searle is elsewhere, to the view that subatomic particles are what's really real, but only to the view that there is a way that things are.

Heidegger likewise affirms that things exist independent of our activity of disclosing them. *According to Searle's definition, then, Heidegger is a realist.* He disavows "realism" only if that means going about trying to prove the existence of the external world or to explain the independence of things in terms of particular theories about them (SZ: 207). Searle too thinks we are wrongheaded to try to prove the existence of the external world, and he insists that his version of realism has nothing to do with "how the world is in fact" (1995: 155). To understand just why these other versions of realism fail, we must draw attention to a distinction both make. Searle maintains he is talking about the condition for intelligibility and not for knowing. His realism, then, comes before epistemology and consequently skepticism. It is a "theory" of ontology not of propositional truths (Searle 1995: 155).

The existence of a way that things are in the world independently of our representations of them is not a truth condition but rather a condition of the form of intelligibility that such statements have. "The point is not epistemic. It is about conditions of intelligibility and not conditions of knowledge, because the point applies whether or not our statements are known or unknown, and whether they are true of false, and even whether the objects purportedly referred to exist or not" (Searle 1995: 187). Heidegger too distinguishes between the condition for understanding and for knowing and takes knowing to be a founded relation on the condition for understanding (SZ: 59–62). Both Searle and Heidegger are confident that they outflank epistemology and skepticism because they are operating on a more fundamental level, ontology. Their realism does not furnish a mechanics of cognition or provide a theory about what in fact is. Rather, their realism identifies the presupposition of every theory.

Now the claim that Searle and Heidegger subscribe to a common realism might seem peculiar since Searle accuses Heidegger of being a relativist, who is not "resolutely anti-idealistic" (2005: 317). He finds an indication of Heidegger's relativism in the denial that there are eternal truths or *de re* propositions. Searle understandably says it is eternally or timelessly true that 2 × 2 = 4, and Heidegger expressly denies the claim. It appears incontestable, then, that Heidegger is making a relativistic claim – or so it seems at first glance. In fact, however, the relativism is an illusion, for Heidegger assigns "true" a different meaning than Searle does: It means fulfilling an intention, uncovering, or manifestation. Now, to be manifest is to be manifest to a dative. Since no dative of manifestation is eternal, no manifestation can be eternal. Given Heidegger's definition of truth, Searle would undoubtedly agree that there are no eternal truths. Put differently, without the being who provides the Background, there can be no propositions, for propositions owe their origin, their utterance, and their confirmation to entities who can intend and ought to do so well. In the absence of such entities, there can simply be no propositions – no true propositions but also no false ones either.[11] Though human entities are not the arbiters of truth, they are a condition for propositions and the normative dimension of truth that grounds them.

At the same time, Heidegger agrees we can access things *de re* even if it is nonsensical to insist that there would be propositions without us. We who intend can recognize that the facts intended in our propositions will endure even if we and our propositions do not.[12] Heidegger insists upon this point in a section Searle cites but apparently misunderstands.[13] "Uncoveredness, truth, unveils an entity precisely as that which it already was beforehand regardless of its uncoveredness and non-uncoveredness. As an uncovered being it becomes intelligible as what is so, how it is and will be, regardless of every possible uncoveredness of itself" (GA24: 314–15, translation modified). Our activity discloses things as existing wholly independently of us and our disclosing. Things have causal powers whether we know of them or not. For instance, feline metabolism would do what feline metabolism does even were we in the dark regarding what it does;

[11] We find in Searle a similar distinction between the true statement, which can perish with us, and the fact stated, which can subsist without us: "Long after we are all dead and there are no statements of any kind, iron will still oxidize; and this is just another way of saying that the fact that iron oxidizes does not depend in any way on the fact that we can state that iron oxidizes. . . . the conditions of possibility of *stating* the facts are not necessarily conditions of possibility of the *existence* of the facts" (Searle 1991: 191).

[12] The human being brings with it understanding and intentionality, a necessary condition for the intelligibility of things. Without human existence, things will still exist but it does not make sense to speak of their intelligibility: "When human existence does not exist, 'independence' 'is' not either, nor 'is' the 'in-itself.' In such a case this sort of thing can be neither understood nor not understood. In such a case even entities within-the-world can neither be discovered nor lie hidden. *In such a case* it cannot be said that entities are, nor can it be said that they are not. But *now*, as long as there is an understanding of being and therefore an understanding of presence-at-hand, it can indeed be said that *in this case* entities will still continue to be" (SZ: 212).

[13] Searle (2005: 332) quotes a passage from this same section to arrive at the opposite interpretation.

and, understanding what it does, we understand that this is what it has been doing all along and will continue to do, whether we want it to or not. According to Heidegger, nature does not need our disclosing to be as it is:

> Uncoveredness, truth, unveils an entity precisely as that which it already was beforehand regardless of its uncoveredness and non-uncoveredness. As an uncovered being it becomes intelligible as that which is just how it is and will be, regardless of every possible uncoveredness. For nature to be as it is, it does not need truth, unveiledness. The composition meant [*Bestand gemmente*] in the true proposition '2 x 2 = 4' can subsist through all eternity without there existing any truth about it. So far as there is a truth about it, this truth understands precisely that nothing in what it means depends on it for being so (GA24: 315).[14]

Nature's intelligibility remains undisturbed whether we are around to understand it or not. And when we are around, we understand it and talk about it fully realizing that it would be what and how it is without our understanding it. In other words, we can know objective reality and understand things *de re* even if, according to Heidegger's vocabulary, an eternal proposition is an absurdity. Searle has missed a certain conceptual relativity between his thought and Heidegger's, but this difference in terms masks a substantial agreement.[15] Searle is right that truth or uncoveredness is relative to human disclosing for Heidegger, but he is wrong to infer that what he, Searle, here calls truth is so relative for Heidegger.[16] Instead, both hold to realism: There is a way that things are that is logically independent of our representations.

Within this agreement, Heidegger emphasizes something essential. Realism is not just about "things," about "the world" and its independence. It necessarily is also about the peculiar feature of our "representations" that they access what is intrinsically independent from them. If we were to deny this character of our representation, as we noted above, realism is indistinguishable from skepticism. Not only does Heidegger affirm realism, but a central aim of his thinking is to show just how this realism is possible. He thinks the "non-dependence [of an entity] precisely in relation to the subject is what is to be explained, to be made as such into a problem" (GA26: 163). Searle misinterprets Heidegger's treatment of representation or disclosedness as a threat to realism when it is in fact

[14] The real can "be as that which in itself it is" even without the existence of human entities and their intending and disclosing (SZ: 212/255).

[15] Searle does allow for a certain conceptual relativity within realism (1995: 155).

[16] In fact, Searle's commitment to a version of the correspondence theory of truth should lead him to deny eternal truths as well: In the absence of intentional states, there can be no correspondence; Searle seems not to be thoroughly consistent regarding his own definition of truth, and sometimes confuses "truth" with its referent, "facts," even though "truth" and "facts" differ in sense. I am thankful to Molly McGrath for this observation.

essential to it. Access is a necessary condition for us to affirm the independence of things. Heidegger names this access “disclosedness,” and Searle does speak somewhat of this access under the rubric, “Background.” Realism, he writes, is “a taken-for-granted part of the Background” (1995: 182). Yet only with Heidegger’s transcendentalism do we have a comprehensive inventory of the conditions for the possibility of the self-showing of things. Heidegger’s transcendentalism, far from destroying the reality of things, instead conspires to safeguard them by bypassing the dialectic of inner and outer, the dialectic that feeds the modern debate between idealism and realism. Heidegger’s question is not *whether* but *how* transcendence occurs.

Is not $2 \times 2 = 4$ timelessly true? The content is, in the sense that we do not confect but discover it as being what it is whether it is discovered or not. But it is not true if there is none to register it as such. This is not, then, an assault upon the reality of things; it is a stipulation that their manifestation entails one to whom they are manifest. This is no mere triviality but instead recognition that an a priori openness to being or transcendence is a necessary condition for things to be manifest in their intelligibility (Golob 2014: 177–78). “If what the term ‘idealism’ says, amounts to the understanding that Being can never be explained by entities but is already that which is ‘transcendental’ for every entity, then idealism affords the only correct possibility for a philosophical problematic. If so, Aristotle was no less an idealist than Kant” (SZ: 208). The modern-day realist may wish to explain the transcendence of being by appeal to the transcendence of entities. Heidegger’s reply is that such so-called realists fail to make room for manifestation or access and thus their realism amounts to a bare assertion: The theme of transcendence safeguards rather than threatens the identity of things. Heidegger’s transcendentalism with its appeal to ontological openness is specified by his fundamental realism about entities. It fills out the condition for the possibility of the transcendence of things relative to the movement of our own transcendence. See Table 6.

Table 6 Making sense of Heidegger’s realism

<table>
<tr><th></th><th>Existentially independent</th><th>Volitionally independent</th><th>Logically independent</th></tr>
<tr><td>Time and clearing</td><td rowspan="2">no</td><td rowspan="3">yes</td><td rowspan="3">yes</td></tr>
<tr><td>Truth and being</td></tr>
<tr><td>Entities and properties</td><td>yes</td></tr>
</table>

The *Res* of Realism and the Question of the *Zusammenhang*

Heidegger's transcendental realism will not excite all realists, for it does not give to us the ability to express timeless truths, and it also suggests that there are different horizons operative for making sense of things at different times, so that Aristotelian nature and Galilean nature open different possibilities of understanding: Even one and the same event, a falling body, for example, admits of multiple, irreducible interpretations (GA41: 89–91). However, Heidegger's transcendental realism does allow us to access things that obtain independent of us as its point of departure and of return. What Heidegger gives us is what I might term "pre-theoretical" realism, an account in which we are fundamentally responsive to the world but without being able to theorize about it once and for all.

Heidegger's realism navigates between two naïve positions. First, it avoids a naïve empiricism according to which all we need to do is open our eyes and we can be privy to an unprejudiced perception of the nature of things. Second, it avoids a naïve rationalism according to which we are endlessly entangled in our own presuppositions and can never access the things themselves. Instead, for Heidegger what is decisive is becoming clear about our way of approach to the things themselves so that we enable them to show themselves from themselves (Golob 2019). We have to frame the topic right, get the context in view, in order to make out the thing in question as it really is.

If something appears colored in the context of white light, it is that color, not absolutely but related to that light. Indeed, it is timelessly true that, given that light, it will appear that color. History is, for Heidegger, a mode of manifestation, analogous to shifting from white to black light. It affects how things appear, what we notice. But it does not alter the existence of the things in question, just their manifestation, nor does it relativize the features that show up in different contexts. Aristotle and Galileo can both access the reality of things despite their conceptual relativity. Yet what something is shows itself more fully given the Aristotelian context with its emphasis on the powers of life. The fact that, for example, our own biology taps into the visible spectrum and that our sun emits white light allows us to register genuine though contextual features of things.

The center of Heidegger's realism is the question of the *Zusammenhang*. In *Being and Time*, in the crucial section 69, Heidegger articulates the fundamental questions of transcendence as follows:

> If we take the temporal Constitution of being-in-the-world as a theme for analysis, we are led to the following questions: in what way is anything like a world possible at all? in what sense *is* the world? what does the world transcend, and how does it do so? how are 'independent' ["unabhängige"]

> entities within-the-world 'connected' ["hängt" ... "zusammen"] with the transcending world? (SZ: 351).

The ecstatic horizonal analysis comprises Heidegger's answer to the question of the *Zusammenhang*. Intentionality is possible in virtue of an a priori ontological context (Golob 2014: 89–90). In the 1935–36 lecture course, published under the title, *The Question Concerning the Thing: On Kant's Doctrine of the Transcendental Principles*, Heidegger says that whenever we enter into the transcendental attitude we can learn this from Kant: There is no isolated thing; rather things belong to a contexture of being, a "between" that we enter into, a between that takes us beyond the thing but also back behind us (GA41: 245). The transcendental attitude focuses on how we can transcend and thereby encounter things (GA41: 181–83). It reveals that we are "the one who always already leaps over things, but in such a way that this leaping over is only possible while things encounter [us] and so remain precisely themselves – while they send us back behind ourselves and our surface" (GA41: 246). Heidegger, in other words, thinks that the choice fruit of the transcendental, whether in Kant (GA41: 239) or Husserl (GA25: 168), is to bring us near to the "contexture" (*Zusammenhang*) of things. In Thomistic terms, it is the question of the *res-aliquid-verum*, the *thing-something-true*, an analysis that considers both the independence and the intrinsic relatedness of the thing, relatedness to other things but also relatedness to us (Aquinas 1952: q. 1, a. 1). See Table 7. Heidegger's transcendence squared with its "contexture of being" (SZ: 216) presupposes as its point of departure the Kantian-Husserlian transcendence and its medieval resonances, a transcendence expressed in SZ 1.1–2 in terms of meaning, context, and truth. The transcendence of being entails the reality of the relations that enable things to be the things they are, replete with their

Table 7 The entity as meaningful, contextual, and unconcealed according to Thomas and Heidegger

	Absolute	**Related but independent of us**	**Related yet dependent on us**
True (*verum*, *wahr*)			yes
Something (*aliquid*, *Zusammenhang*)		yes	
Thing (*res*, *Ding*)	yes		

characteristic causal intelligibility. This transcendence stands at the midpoint: It enables us to make sense of entities in their transcendent otherness and, more interestingly, it in turn is enabled by the origin of experience in being appropriated. The "between" and "contexture" that emerges through transcendental thinking is taken up into Heidegger's own mature thinking on the question of the place of the human and the thing. Prior to the relation of self and thing, "the human being in his essence is ek-sistent into the openness of being, into the open-region that first clears the 'between' within which a 'relation' of subject to object can 'be'" (GA9: 350/266). What is the relation of the open-region to releasement on the one hand and the relation of the open-region to the thing on the other? Heidegger says that the relation is one of "enregioning" (*die Vergegnis*) and "bethinging" (*die Bedingnis*) (GA77: 139–40). The world is a contexture that encompasses us and things.

5 Appropriating Transcendence

One says that Heidegger disavows his transcendentalism. Yet in truth he remains committed to the priority of relatedness and the language of presence and absence, though he ever experiments with novel forms of expression more adequate to its dynamic. His principal foe is what transcendentalism merely *seems* to do rather than what it in fact does. His legitimate concern is that transcendence, in leading us into its terminus, eliminates the need for any further transcendencies. To step beyond subject and object is to come to a stop and abide in the truth of being. But to fulfil something is in fact a way of remaining with something. In keeping with the principle, *a potiori fit denominatio* (SZ: 329), and in reflecting on the fact that one can only arrive at one's destination by means of taking a first step, "transcendental" remains the necessary first approach to Heidegger's lasting topic and it therefore retains its legitimacy as a permanent albeit imperfect name for his thinking. The "transcendental" tradition also remains the clearest precursor in the history of philosophy to his own approach. Heidegger's transcendentalism is not a phase in his thinking but his one lasting topic named from the first approach all must take. There is no term apart from the movement, no homecoming without a going out.

The figure of the path or way is central to Heidegger's thinking, from his early reflections on method as the way into the subject matter to the preoccupation with the right way of expressing the turn. His most comprehensive anthology of essays is called *Pathmarks*, *Wegmarken*, and his most aptly named anthology is named for paths that lead into the forest, *Holzwege*. Heraclitus said the way up and the way down are one and the same, but Aristotle, in the *Nicomachean Ethics*, noted that Plato was troubled about the turn from the way up to the way down.

> Let us not fail to notice, however, that there is a difference between arguments from and those to the first principles. For Plato, too, was right in raising this question and asking, as he used to do, "are we on the way from or to the first principles?" There is a difference, as there is in a race-course between the course from the judges to the turning-point and the way back. For, while we must begin with what is known, things are objects of knowledge in two senses – some to us, some without qualification. Presumably, then, we must begin with things known to us (1941: 1.4).

Here Heidegger proves to be Platonic in his attentions. The way up is transcendental, a matter of stepping or going beyond; the way down is a matter of returning home, of in-abiding or dwelling. What is first for us is not what is first in itself; our stepping beyond comes back to rest with that which is naturally first. Our act of transcendence loses itself in the movement of experience itself.

Heidegger advances a new reading of Kant in terms of the between in order to gesture toward his own more comprehensive investigations; the transcendental tradition, despite its limits, remains the nearest anticipation of his own peculiar transcendentalism. He holds to phenomenological seeing and the transcendental domain but experiments with nonmetaphysical modes of speaking to avoid two unwanted appearances, namely that being is an object opposite the subject and that the horizon is anchored in the subject. He moves within transcendentalism from a language of horizon to a language of affectivity, from temporality to historicity, from stepping beyond to stepping back, from understanding to releasement.

The judgment, "The waves are big today," is true if and only if the waves are in fact big this day. In this way, thinking about judgments can easily lead one to focus on the question of their correctness, on whether they match or fit the facts. Yet the transcendental interest wishes to call attention to something we overlook in our ordinary and understandable concern for whether judgments we register or judgments we hear are correct or incorrect, and that is the wondrous fit between language and thing. How do our words reach out beyond us to present the very belonging together of subject and predicate? The condition for the possibility of truth is the self-showing of a state of affairs, a self-showing let be by our speech.

This transcendence (T^1) is the transcendence Heidegger finds at the heart of the transcendental attitude deployed in the *Critique of Pure Reason* and on display especially in the highest principle of synthetic judgments, which endeavors to elucidate just how our thoughts can reach beyond themselves in order to articulate the givenness of things as opposed to the highest principle of analytic judgment, which, for Kant, has to do with our thoughts alone. For T^1

focuses neither on the judgment as in logic nor on the object as with everyday concern or scientific interest but instead seeks to fathom the mysterious origin of their belonging together, an origin that Heidegger dubs the "between" or "contexture" precisely in order to indicate the nonsubjective and nonobjective character of the transcendental domain.

Yet all of this belongs to T^1, not T^2, which is to say it is at once adapted by Heidegger insofar as it provides the point of departure for his own project and insofar as it provides an exemplar for a type of thinking of a back and forth relatedness. The chief difference is that the "between" shifts from the transcendental movement of self to thing at work in Kant and other exemplars of the transcendental tradition to the transcendental movement of our relation to the between itself. For consider: we have been talking about things since there has been human existence yet only slowly did we surmise the source of our ability to do so. Heidegger urges us to see that we stop prematurely at the first transcendental horizon, for right at its term when it unearths the hidden presupposition of the "between" is there the opportunity to unfold that very "between" in a more expansive and comprehensive manner as the opening up of world in the affectivity of being. Heidegger's transcendentalism, he says, is a transcendentalism of a higher power, T^2. Instead of bringing the subject–predicate relation back to the subject–object relation, he brings the transcendent subject–predicate relation back through the transcending subject–object relation to the transcendental horizon of world, self, and thing. We are able to meet with entities thanks to the opening up of the open "between." The a priori remains, but it is no longer a purely formal a priori but is instead a material one and therefore is historical in character.

Heidegger speaks of the path into the forest clearing, but we could also speak of being cast into the sea. All of our casting of nets or our casting of ourselves into the surf can happen only because of the original casting, even though our casting will always fall short of the original casting. Hence there can be no metaphysics of the casting but only a phenomenological and affective recovery of the originary casting. Taking something as something happens within an act of transcendence opened up by the experienced unfurling of world. The world casts itself open temporally (and spatially), and we find ourselves within the casting; all our casting takes its bearing from the principal casting open. "S is p" can be cast by us due to our first being cast into a world in which things can be encountered in their relentless waves of significance. Relationality comes to the fore in the transcendental consideration.

Horizon as Definitive

At the heart of Heidegger's real worries concerning his transcendentalism is the supposition that the horizon stands open only because of our activity rather than being a condition for our own experience. In this supposition transcendence seems closed to history and takes its bearing solely from the present. Yet this supposition seems to be no true appearance but only an illusion; it is a mistake to think of the horizon as carrying these implications, for the horizon, both in its philosophical and its everyday meaning, always constitutes the border between that which is present and that which is absent, a border that we do not project but find inescapably bounding our field of experience.

In its everyday sense, horizon situates us. The sun sets relative to my vantage point, but I have to get there into the clearing in order to see it. Yet it is also an invitation to my freedom, to head out toward the horizon, which ever recedes before me. We cannot catch up to the horizon, which remains forever elusive, and this is precisely because the horizon is not a thing, nor is it simply the presence of what is present; rather its elusiveness consists precisely in its being constituted by both presence and absence. Indeed, Husserl adopts the term for phenomenology to name the border between presence and absence (Sokolowski 1978). The perceived thing, for example, bears a horizon that solicits my attention, that calls for me, and elicits my movement. Come, it tells me, consider my other side. Hence the horizon is not a limit on the present but a gesture toward the absent: "This leaving open, prior to further determinings (which perhaps never take place), is a moment included in the given consciousness itself; it is precisely what makes up the 'horizon'" (Husserl, 1977: 45). And without that gesture or summons to the absent, there would be no presence, no sense of the presence as fulfilling that summons. Horizon names the phenomenological finis of finitude. As Renxiang Liu (2024) argues, the concept of horizon comes to the fore in Heidegger's interpretation of Kant but not in such a way that it remains bound to a conception of projection; instead, horizon determines the self rather than being determined by the self. Releasement, then, is key to making sense of Heidegger's nonsubjective transcendental philosophy in which horizon is not projected but allowed to unfold. In this way, Heidegger has no good reason to censure or supress the use of "horizon."

But what of history? It is not accidental that Nietzsche reaches for the term horizon when speaking of the advantage and disadvantage of history for life (SZ: 396). In fact, historicity is impossible to express without something equivalent to the concept of horizon. Only if the complex alters is history philosophically interesting. Heidegger's motivational story about the fateful flaw of the Greek horizon, which engenders the medieval, then the modern, and finally the contemporary horizon, cannot be understood apart from horizon-talk. The claim that the Greeks could not fail to overlook the original experience of truth as disclosedness involves a finitude that finds expression in the terminology of horizon. How can things appear different from age to age without some modalization of the whole? And how can this modalization be clearly expressed without reference to changes in horizon? It was not for nothing that Heidegger's student, Gadamer, chose the terminology of "fusion of horizons" to make sense of our ability to make sense of that which is other, to accommodate our own vantage point to that of another time or place or person (Gadamer 1989: 306–7).

Horizon names the border between presence and absence, a border that percolates in all of our speech about things (Engelland 2021b). The horizon establishes our vantage point and unfolds relative to that vantage point but not in such a way that it is a function of our vantage point. Instead, it is quite the opposite. Only because the horizon horizons, only because the presence slides into absence is it possible for there to be vantage points. Hence, Heidegger cannot avoid implicitly making use of horizon, and he has no good reason to jettison it.[17] It is the transcendental horizon, after all, that names the terminus of his thinking. "The horizon is no longer what is 'seen' in advance so as then to be 'projected onto'; rather, it is what presubjectively orients every projection according to the way beings (things and events) unfold themselves in the fullness of time and at their own paces" (Liu 2024: 236).

The Transcendental Properties of Being

Heidegger, taking a cue from Aristotle's reading of his predecessors, fits the whole history of philosophy into a narrative in which all conspire unsuccessfully to work out the project for the first time worked out as such by Heidegger. Yet, without in any way wishing to question the real worth of Heidegger's insight, including its genuine novelty, one must point out that it hardly comprises the essence of philosophy; it hardly recapitulates, without remainder, the

[17] In a 1938–39 lecture course on *The Advantages and Disadvantages of History for Life*, Heidegger asks of Nietzsche's use of the term, "The horizon and the perspective-character of life (cf. no. 119). The projection of the horizon [*Gesichtskreisentwurf*] – its breadth and extent –, *how is this determined*?" (GA46: 137). Heidegger will argue that the horizon is projected by life, that is, by the will to power, the fulfillment of metaphysics. Here one hears an echo of Heidegger's metaphysics of transcendence from a decade earlier. However, while the perceptual horizon can plausibly (though mistakenly) be understood as something projected by the living thing, the historical horizon cannot. The truth of the matter is that both perception and history happen thanks to the setting of the horizon, that is, its withdrawal from our awareness; neither is simply projected. We are cast into hidden horizons rather than originally casting them.

whole of the philosophical enterprise. Philosophy is enriched but not replaced by Heidegger's affective transcendentalism.

In the *Critique of Pure Reason*, Kant refers to the transcendental philosophy of the ancients, and Heidegger, too, in *Being and Time* and elsewhere, engages in Thomas's elucidation of the transcendentals in reference to Aristotle's definition of the rational soul as in a way all things. I would like to conclude this study of Heidegger and the transcendental by making a twofold case: First, that Heidegger makes a singular contribution to the transcendental tradition, and, second, that Heidegger's transcendentalism could be improved by taking on a bit more of that tradition.[18]

As to the first, Heidegger rightly criticizes the transcendental tradition for a lack of clarity regarding the dynamic interrelation of truth and being. His working out, after Husserl, of the interplay of presence and absence that is constitutive of experience, an interplay rooted in the primal dynamics of original temporality, is profound and inescapably true. In that way, the peculiar openness of the human vis-à-vis everything else is brought to a kind of halcyon clarity. Heidegger gives us an account of transcendence that decisively undercuts modern epistemology and its monomaniacal focus on inward immanence; it returns our minds to the shared world in which things emerge from out of a contexture, constituted by a field of relations rooted in temporality.

As to the second, however, the openness in Heidegger's hands ossifies. To make the case, we need only turn to Thomas's derivation of the transcendentals in *De veritate*, 1, 1. Thomas distinguishes between two sorts of transcendentals: those absolutely considered and those considered in relation. Of those attributes that are absolutely considered, which hold independent of a relation to anything else, Thomas says that each being is *unum* and *res*. Now, we can also consider entities in relation, either to other entities in general or to the rational soul in particular. It is only in reference to the possible relatedness to the rational soul that entities are *verum* and *bonum*. Thomas does not shy away from stating the obvious corollary: If, on the impossible supposition, there were no intellective soul, there would be no truth. Yet, even if there were no truth, there would still be a unity and native intelligibility to things. In light of medieval transcendentalism, we can see in Heidegger a peculiar ambiguity. On the one hand, he insists that we are open in our being to the being of things and to being itself. On the other, he does not permit us to ascribe to things an intelligibility to meet with as a result of this openness. If we are genuinely open, then we ought to be open to

[18] Dahlstrom says that Heidegger's failed efforts to derive the various meanings of being from the horizon of human existence stems from his attempt to bridge the medieval and modern transcendentalism (2015: 100, n. 9). My view is that the attempt to do so is precisely the task put to us by history: to remedy the defects of both traditions in light of the strengths of the other.

what things are independent of that openness; if we are not genuinely open, then there is no sense of making a pretence to such openness. Heidegger is right that the tradition fails to distinguish sufficiently that which is present from presence, and therein lies his transcendental genius, but he is wrong to think that the tradition's focus on intelligibility is undermined as a result. Instead, Heidegger's transcendentalism sets intelligibility free to become a topic in its own right. This, I take it, explains why Edith Stein, who likewise emphasizes such openness, should become obsessed with intelligibility in her alternative exploration of the meaning of being: *Finite and Eternal Being: An Attempt at an Ascent to the Meaning of Being* (2002), a book whose title is meant to indicate a challenge to Heidegger's temporal horizon as definitive for understanding.

Heidegger's later worry about transcendentalism, namely that it makes it appear that the horizon appears only relative to us, is an effect of his having tried to think relatedness without a corresponding absolute consideration. His concern, then, is an effect of a certain modern version of transcendentalism. For example, when Kant says, in the *Prolegomena*, that the categories of human understanding are the letters thanks to which we can read the phenomena, he is expressing the limits of modern transcendentalism: The only order we can experience is the order that we ourselves project (Rosemann 2015: 61). This is a direct expression of the *mathesis universalis* as articulated in Descartes's *Rules for the Direction of our Native Intelligence*: Even if there is no natural order, I will establish an order relative to me. The transcendentalism of Thomas had the great innovation of making truth relative to us but only insofar as the *res* was emphatically not so relative. When Bonaventure says, in the *Collationes*, that in understanding the texture of things we read a text that we ourselves did not compose, he expresses a nonmodern transcendentalism (Rosemann 2015: 38–42). Heidegger's own thinking moves from being more closely aligned with modern transcendentalism to being more closely aligned with the medieval. More precisely, he remains nostalgic for something that eludes the projection of the *mathesis universalis*, but he wishes not to thematize that something by itself either as *res* simpliciter or as *res* relative to the eternal origin of existence; instead he resolutely or doggedly remains within the horizon of temporal and historical finitude, catching glimpses of the transcendence of the thing through the changing horizons of being.

My own view is that Heidegger's transcendentalism gives the ultimate account of experience, thankfully avoiding the short-circuit of onto-theology, which seeks to explain presence causally and in so doing bypasses the essence of what is to be explained. At the same time, I think there is more to think about regarding the independence of the entities we encounter that is fathomed relative to the horizon of our experience, and here there is a genuine place for raising causal questions. Other philosophical methods and inquiries are suited for the investigation of these avenues (Schmitz 2005; Sokolowski 2008; Wood, 2015a; Engelland 2020c).

Theses on Heidegger

(1) Transcendentalism is the clearest and most compelling expression of his one path.
   (a) It draws from what Heidegger sees as the high-water mark of the philosophical tradition in the ancients, the medievals, and Kant.
   (b) It articulates a novel philosophical program which complements the tradition.
   (c) It involves a *logos* clearly differentiated from a *mythos*, a *logos* that can be translated into other tongues.

(2) Heidegger comes to have legitimate but delimited worries about its clear and compelling expression.
   (a) Those who view these worries as entailing a rejection operate in an understanding of truth as correctness, which is other than Heidegger's own (SZ: 214–19). Heidegger's transcendentalism is neither correct nor incorrect; it is his first halting expression of his breakthrough, whose very effectiveness enables the subsequent assessment of its ultimate inadequacy.
   (b) These worries concern various illusions, or skewed appearances. First, the illusion of a horizon open opposite a subject; second, the impression that being is an object opposite time; third, the scholarly view that Heidegger is reducible to either Kant or Husserl.
   (c) But Heidegger's transcendentalism never endorsed any of these positions.
   (d) Of course, there is a shift of emphasis from projection to thrownness, understanding to affectivity, and with it a shift from a language imposed on experience to a language that constitutes experience. But the shift from the anxiety of *Being and Time* to the terror of the *Contributions* is nothing but a change of emphasis, designed to underscore the fact that experience happens through us rather than because of us.
   (e) Heidegger, in other words, fine-tunes and completes but does not abandon his transcendentalism.

(3) Yet Heidegger remains a (merely) transcendental thinker.
   (a) That is, he thinks about how the determinate play of presence and absence in life and history makes possible the experience of making sense of things.
   (b) He summons us to take heed of this condition and not neglect it.

(c) But he does not clarify any number of perennial philosophical topics concerning such things as natural essences rather than just presences, ultimate causes rather than just grounds, and personal responsibilities rather than just appropriations.
(d) Heidegger's transcendentalism is his greatest achievement, though it has limits he recognized – and still further ones he did not.

Why Heidegger's Transcendentalism Now?

The burden of justifying any engagement with Heidegger has only increased. Not only do the old charges apply of his being professionally unclear and personally unkind but now we have ample evidence he harbored despicable opinions (Farin and Malpas 2016). Can Heidegger's philosophy be separated from his deplorable life? If not, we are obliged to avoid it altogether lest we too succumb to its dangerous spell. It is precisely here at Heidegger's weakest point, however, that his transcendentalism recommends itself. How so?

First, Heidegger's transcendentalism is manifestly in continuity with Husserl's, and therefore it belongs within the horizon of transcendental phenomenology. It is cosmopolitan and not parochial. Second, Heidegger's falling prey to parochial ideology in the 1930s happens in tandem with his distancing himself from such cosmopolitan transcendentalism. Third, in the second half of the 1920s, when Heidegger developed his transcendental phenomenology, he never tires of repeating that the transcendental project does not furnish us with a worldview and could not provide any directives for how to live life. Hence, Heidegger's transcendentalism, as a phenomenological explication of the condition for the possibility of experience, is not the entirety of philosophy or of wisdom. That its practitioner should have failed to be exemplary in his words and deeds does not call into question transcendentalism, because transcendentalism is not a way of life, something that can only be established by raising the question of the natural human good (Velkley 2011: 95).

We can learn from Heidegger's appropriation of transcendental phenomenology while recognizing its limits: It does not help us know how to live and precisely insofar as it does not, but only insofar as it does not, it offers no immunity to worldviews and ideologies, including nationalism and racism. For that, we must carry our thoughts along different paths. Heidegger's transcendentalism is the highpoint of Heidegger's thought and a highpoint in the transcendental tradition. It provides indispensable help for our own efforts to make sense of experience as that which affords the possibility of making sense of things. Yet there is more to philosophy than the transcendental, as important as it may be.

For thirty-five years scholars have had the unenviable task of working through the posthumous manuscripts and notebooks that read at times like Heidegger's attempt to do what Wittgenstein argued was impossible, namely invent a private language. Yet with the theme of transcendentalism, with the theme of the working out of the condition for the possibility of making sense of things and of making sense of such making sense, we have a theme that is intelligible, novel, and salutary. Heidegger's transcendentalism allows him to explain normativity in a way that has advantages over its alternatives (Crowell and Malpas 2007; Crowell 2013; Golob 2014; Engelland 2015; Engelland 2020b; Burch and McMullin 2020). In particular, the care structure and call of conscience afford a powerful dynamic for the claim of truth, renewed by the affectivity of being. Philosophers of whatever stripe, including those who are to come, will surely want to help themselves to such a gift. If there is sense to the later esoteric writings, it comes only by way of a modification of the articulated transcendentalism. If there is real innovation in Heidegger, it is to be found in his account of experiencing the truth of the truth of things. If there is a gift that Heidegger can make to our understanding, it is principally and primarily his transcendentalism, squared.

Coda: Transcendence in English

Heidegger, we know, looks to the German poet Hölderlin to find a new vocabulary to articulate the domain that first disclosed itself transcendentally and hence can be termed the transcendental domain. Yet given my contention that transcendentalism is a cosmopolitan theme that can find expression in any tongue, I might do well to produce a poet writing in neither German nor Greek that renews the transcendental vocabulary.

The English poet Gerard Manley Hopkins, SJ, penned the suggestive poem, "My own heart let me more have pity on" (1918: 110–11). I bracket whatever biographical or psychological factors may have been at play during the poet's dark mood and propose to offer a phenomenological and transcendental reading of the poem itself. It begins as follows:

> My own heart let me more have pity on; let
> Me live to my sad self hereafter kind,
> Charitable; not live this tormented mind
> With this tormented mind tormenting yet.

The poem invites the heart to be heartfelt to itself. The problem of the disaffection arises from a failure of affectivity, a failure to turn from the machinations of mind to the spring of affectivity. The poem presents the to-fro structure of tormenting and being tormented as the function of an uprooted thought and its ego. The next four lines express this powerfully.

> I cast for comfort I can no more get
> By groping round my comfortless, than blind
> Eyes in their dark can day or thirst can find
> Thirst's all-in-all in all a world of wet.

What is comfort? Not the lack of strain, for we do not strain for a cessation of straining; rather comfort is the distinguishing mark of home: all the comforts of home. From out of the experience of homelessness or alienation, the poem speaks of casting or projecting or hurling comfort but notes the vanity of doing so. We get comfort and the experience of being at home not by generating them but by receiving them. The poem likens the impossibility of willing to feel at home to two similar situations, one spatial and cognitive, the other temporal and affective: blind eyes cannot make the night day, for sight is receptive to light rather than casting it, and thirst cannot find its once and for all satisfaction in a world of liquid, for thirst returns again and again for the water of this world. The ego, like the eyes and thirst, is marked by a radical poverty of being.

Now the poem shifts. At first, it addressed the heart, then the poverty of the ego, and now it addresses the soul or self. It invites the "Jackself" or the familiar everyday self that is jaded by the homelessness of this world to "let be."

> Soul, self; come, poor Jackself, I do advise
> You, jaded, let be; call off thoughts awhile
> Elsewhere; leave comfort root-room; let joy size
> At God knows when to God knows what; whose smile
> 's not wrung, see you; unforeseen times rather – as skies
> Betweenpie mountains – lights a lovely mile.

What might our jaded Jackselves let be? We are to let joy grow from out of its mysterious source and toward its mysterious end. That affectivity is not "wrung," not wrested, not seized from experience by our agency; rather it happens to us when it does, because we let it happen. We cannot produce the requisite affectivity; we can only prepare for it by making room for it to take root.

The poem speaks of an open space, not a forest clearing, but a skyscape, stretching between mountains, and illuminating the "pied" or colourful patchwork of clouds. That encompassing display overtakes us, gladdens us, and affords a welcome refuge from the sterility of our unaffected thoughts. According to the words of the poet, then, we are cast casters who do well to let be and let our affectivity take root and in doing so find meaning – the comfort of home – for all our casting. Transcendentalism is not ultimately rooted in the casting of thought but instead in affectivity, the being cast of the heart. As such, we can find room for all the things that appear against the horizon of the cheering sky. The between is no empty, homeless between, for its lit display is pied, spotted, dappled – with things.

Texts and Method of Citation

All references to Heidegger's writings are to the standard edition of *Being and Time* (*Sein und Zeit*, see below) or to the respective volume of the *Complete Edition* (*Gesamtausgabe*) of his writings. References to *Sein und Zeit* are cited as 'SZ' followed by the page number, for example, 'SZ: 15'; references to volumes of the *Gesamtausgabe* are cited as 'GA' followed by the volume number, colon, and page number, for example, 'GA55: 19'. Most English translations include the pagination of the German original, making it possible to dispense with citing the translations' pagination. For any exceptions the German pagination is given followed by a slash and the pagination of the English translation, for example, 'GA9: 106/84'.

SZ — *Sein und Zeit*, 18th ed. Tübingen: Max Niemeyer Verlag, 2001. English translation: *Being and Time*. Translated by John Macquarrie and Edward Robinson. New York: Harper & Row, 1962.

GA3 — *Kant und das Problem der Metaphysik*. Edited by Friedrich-Wilhelm von Herrmann. Frankfurt am Main: Vittorio Klostermann, 1991. English translation: *Kant and the Problem of Metaphysics*, 4th ed. Translated by Richard Taft. Bloomington, IN: Indiana University Press, 1996.

GA9 — *Wegmarken*. Edited by Friedrich-Wilhelm von Herrmann. Frankfurt am Main: Klostermann, 1976. English translation: *Pathmarks*. Edited by William McNeill. Cambridge: Cambridge University Press, 1998.

GA12 — *Unterwegs zur Sprache*. Edited by Friedrich-Wilhelm von Herrmann. Frankfurt am Main: Klostermann, 1985. English translation: "A Dialogue on Language." In *On the Way to Language*. Translated by Peter D. Hertz. New York: Harper & Row, 1971.

GA17 — *Einführung in die phänomenologische Forschung*. Edited by Friedrich-Wilhelm von Herrmann. Frankfurt am Main: Klostermann, 1994. English translation: *Introduction to Phenomenological Research*. Translated by Daniel O. Dahlstrom. Bloomington, IN: Indiana University Press, 2005.

GA18 — *Grundbegriffe der aristotelischen Philosophie*. Edited by Mark Michalski. Frankfurt am Main: Vittorio Klostermann, 2002. English translation: *Basic Concepts of Aristotelian Philosophy*.

Translated by Robert D. Metcalf and Mark B. Tanzer. Bloomington, IN: Indiana University Press, 2009.

GA19 *Platon: Sophistes*. Edited by Ingeborg Schüßler. Frankfurt am Main: Vittorio Klostermann, 1992. English translation: *Plato's 'Sophist'*. Translated by Richard Rojcewicz and André Schuwer. Bloomington, IN: Indiana University Press, 1997.

GA20 *Prolegomena zur Geschichte des Zeitbegriffs*. Edited by Petra Jaeger. Frankfurt am Main: Vittorio Klostermann, 1979. English translation: *History of the Concept of Time: Prolegomena*. Translated by Theodore Kisiel. Bloomington, IN: Indiana University Press, 1985.

GA21 *Logik: Die Frage nach der Wahrheit*. Edited by Walter Biemel. Frankfurt am Main: Vittorio Klostermann, 1976. English translation: *Logic: The Question of Truth*. Translated by Thomas Sheehan. Bloomington, IN: Indiana University Press, 2010.

GA22 *Grundbegriffe der antiken Philosophie*. Edited by Franz-Karl Blust. Frankfurt am Main: Vittorio Klostermann, 1993. English translation: *Basic Concepts of Ancient Philosophy*. Translated by Richard Rojcewicz. Bloomington, IN: Indiana University Press, 2008.

GA24 *Die Grundprobleme der Phänomenologie*. Edited by Friedrich-Wilhelm von Herrmann. Frankfurt am Main: Vittorio Klostermann, 1975. English translation: *The Basic Problems of Phenomenology*, rev. ed. Translated by Albert Hofstadter. Bloomington, IN: Indiana University Press, 1982.

GA25 *Phänomenologische Interpretation von Kants Kritik der reinen Vernunft*. Edited by Ingtraud Görland. Frankfurt am Main: Vittorio Klostermann, 1977. English translation: *Phenomenological Interpretations of Kant's* Critique of Pure Reason. Translated by Parvis Emad and Kenneth Maly. Bloomington, IN: Indiana University Press, 1997.

GA26 *Metaphysische Anfangsgründe der Logik im Ausgang von Leibniz. Gesamtausgabe* 26. Edited by Klaus Held. Frankfurt am Main: Vittorio Klostermann, 1978. English translation: *The Metaphysical Foundations of Logic*. Translated by Michael Heim. Bloomington, IN: Indiana University Press, 1984.

GA29/30 *Die Grundbegriffe der Metaphysik. Welt–Endlichket–Einsamkeit*. Edited by Friedrich-Wilhelm von Herrmann. Frankfurt am Main: Vittorio Klostermann, 1983. English translation: *The Fundamental Concepts of Metaphysics*.

Translated by William McNeill and Nicholas Walker. Bloomington, IN: Indiana University Press, 1995.

GA31 *Vom Wesen der menschlichen Freiheit: Einleitung in die Philosophie*. Edited by Hartmut Tietjen. Frankfurt am Main: Vittorio Klostermann, 1982. English translation: *The Essence of Human Freedom: An Introduction to Philosophy*. London: Continuum, 2002.

GA33 *Aristoteles,* Metaphysik Theta *1–3: Von Wesen und Wirklichkeit der Kraft*. Edited by Heinrich Hüni. Frankfurt am Main: Vittorio Klostermann, 1981. English translation: *Aristotle's Metaphysics Theta 1–3: On the Essence and Actuality of Force*. Translated by Walter Brogan and Peter Warnek. Bloomington, IN: Indiana University Press, 1995.

GA41 *Die Frage nach dem Ding: Zu Kants Lehre von den transzendentalen Grundsätzen*. Edited by Petra Jaeger. Frankfurt am Main: Vittorio Klostermann, 1984. English translation: *The Question Concerning the Thing: On Kant's Doctrine of the Transcendental Principles*. Translated by James. D. Reid and Benjamin D. Crowe. London: Rowman & Littlefield International, 2018.

GA45 *Grundfragen der Philosophie: Ausgewählte 'Probleme' der 'Logik.'* Edited by Friedrich-Wilhelm von Herrmann. Frankfurt am Main: Vittorio Klostermann, 1984. English translation: *Basic Questions of Philosophy: Selected 'Problems' of 'Logic.'* Translated by Richard Rojcewicz and André Schuwer. Bloomington, IN: Indiana University Press, 1994.

GA46 *Zur Auslegung von Nietzsches II. Unzeitgemäßer Betrachtung*. Edited by Hans-Joachim Friedrich. Frankfurt am Main: Vittorio Klostermann, 2003. English translation: *Interpretation of Nietzsche's Second Untimely Meditation*. Translated by Ullrich Haase and Mark Sinclair. Bloomington, IN: Indiana University Press, 2016.

GA65 *Beiträge zur Philosophie (Vom Ereignis)*. Edited by Friedrich-Wilhelm von Herrmann. Frankfurt am Main: Vittorio Klostermann, 1989. English translation: *Contributions to Philosophy (From Enowning)*. Translated by Parvis Emad and Kenneth Maly. Bloomington, IN: Indiana University Press, 1999.

GA77 *Feldweg-Gespräche*. Edited by Ingrid Schüssler. Frankfurt am Main: Vittorio Klostermann, 1995. English translation: *Country Path Conversations*. Translated by Bret W. Davis. Bloomington, IN: Indiana University Press, 2016.

GA82 *Zu eigenen Veröffentlichungen*. Edited by Friedrich-Wilhelm von Herrmann. Frankfurt am Main: Vittorio Klostermann, 2018.

GA94 *Überlegungen II-VI (Schwarze Hefte 1931–1938)*. Edited by Peter Trawny. Frankfurt am Main: Vittorio Klostermann, 2014. English translation: *Ponderings II-VI: Black Notebooks 1931–1938*. Translated by Richard Rojcewicz. Bloomington, IN: Indiana University Press, 2016.

I have modified English translations without comment in order to render a consistent and readable technical vocabulary:

appropriation	*Ereignis*
leap	*Sprung*
human existence	*Dasein*
being	*Sein*
be-ing	*Seyn*
entities	*Seiendes*
handiness	*Zuhandenheit*
on-handness	*Vorhandenheit*
temporality	*Temporalität*
timeliness	*Zeitlichkeit*
bringing forth	*Zeitigung*

References

Aquinas, Thomas. (1952). *Truth*, tr. Robert W. Mulligan. S.J. Chicago, IL: Henry Regnery Company.

Aristotle. (1941). *Nicomachean Ethics*. In *Basic Works*, ed. Richard McKeon. New York: Random House.

Braver, Lee. (2015). "Turning from a Given Horizon to the Givenness of Horizons." In *Division III of Heidegger's 'Being and Time': The Unanswered Question of Being*, ed. Lee Braver, 57–82. Cambridge, MA: MIT Press.

Burch, Matthew and Irene McMullin, editors. (2020). *Transcending Reason: Heidegger on Rationality*. London: Rowman & Littlefield International.

Carman, Taylor. (2003). *Heidegger's Analytic: Interpretation, Discourse, and Authenticity in 'Being and Time'*. Cambridge: Cambridge University Press.

Crowell, Steven. (2013). *Normativity and Phenomenology in Husserl and Heidegger*. Cambridge: Cambridge University Press.

Crowell, Steven and Jeff Malpas. (2007). *Transcendental Heidegger*. Stanford, CA: Stanford University Press.

Dahlstrom, Daniel. (1991). "Heidegger's Kantian Turn: Notes to His Commentary on the 'Kritik Der Reinen Vernunft'." *The Review of Metaphysics* 45: 329–361.

Dahlstrom, Daniel. (2001). *Heidegger's Concept of Truth*. Cambridge: Cambridge University Press.

Dahlstrom, Daniel. (2005). "Heidegger's Transcendentalism." *Research in Phenomenology* 35: 29–54.

Dahlstrom, Daniel. (2015). "The End of Fundamental Ontology." In *Division III of Heidegger's 'Being and Time': The Unanswered Question of Being*, ed. Lee Braver, 83–103. Cambridge, MA: MIT Press.

Engelland, Chad. (2004). "Marcel and Heidegger on the Proper Matter and Manner of Thinking." *Philosophy Today* 48: 91–106.

Engelland, Chad. (2010). "Unmasking the Person." *International Philosophical Quarterly* 50: 447–460.

Engelland, Chad. (2015). "Heidegger and the Human Difference." *Journal of the American Philosophical Association* 1: 175–193.

Engelland, Chad. (2017). *Heidegger's Shadow: Kant, Husserl, and the Transcendental Turn*. London: Routledge Press.

Engelland, Chad. (2020a). *Phenomenology*. Cambridge, MA: MIT Press.

Engelland, Chad. (2020b). "Grice and Heidegger on the Logic of Conversation." In *Transcending Reason: Heidegger's Transformation of Phenomenology*, ed. Matt Burch and Irene McMullin, 171–186. New Heidegger Research. London: Rowman & Littlefield International.

Engelland, Chad. (2020c). "Three Versions of the Question, 'Why Is There Something Rather than Nothing?'" *Proceedings of the American Catholic Philosophical Association* 94: 73–89.

Engelland, Chad. (2021a). "Phenomenology at the Beach." *Philosophy Now* 144: 36.

Engelland, Chad. (2021b). "Inflecting 'Presence' and 'Absence': On Sharing the Phenomenological Conversation." In *Language and Phenomenology*, ed. Chad Engelland, 273–295. London: Routledge Press.

Farin, Ingo and Jeff Malpas, editors. (2016). *Heidegger's* 'Black Notebooks' (1931–1941). Cambridge, MA: MIT Press.

Gadamer, Hans-Georg. (1989). *Truth and Method*, 2d ed., tr. Joel Weinsheimer and Conald G. Marshall. New York: Continuum.

Golob, Sacha. (2014). *Heidegger on Concepts, Freedom and Normativity*. Cambridge: Cambridge University Press.

Golob, Sacha. (2019). "Was Heidegger a Relativist?" In *The Emergence of Relativism: German Thought from the Enlightenment to National Socialism*, ed. Martin Kusch, Katherina Kinzel, Johannes Steizinger, and Niels Wildschut, 181–95. New York: Routledge.

Herrmann, Friedrich-Wilhelm. (2022). *Hermeneutics and Reflection: Heidegger and Husserl on the Concept of Phenomenology*. Toronto: University of Toronto Press.

Hopkins, Gerard Manley. (1918). *Poems*, ed. Robert Bridges. London: Oxford University Press.

Husserl, Edmund. (1977). *Cartesian Meditations: An Introduction to Phenomenol ogy*, tr. Dorion Cairns. The Hague: Martinus Nijhoff.

Husserl, Edmund. (2014). *Ideas for a Pure Phenomenology and Phenomenological Philosophy: First Book: General Introduction to Pure Phenomenology*, tr. Daniel O. Dahlstrom. Indianapolis, IN: Hackett Publishing.

Kinkaid, James. (2019). "Phenomenology, Idealism, and the Legacy of Kant." *British Journal for the History of Philosophy* 27 (3), 593–614.

Kisiel, Theodore. (1973). "The Mathematical and the Hermeneutical: On Heidegger's Notion of the Apriori." In *Martin Heidegger: In Europe and America*, ed. Edward G. Ballard and Charles E. Scott, 109–20. The Hague: Martinus Nijhoff.

Kisiel, Theodore. (1993). *The Genesis of Heidegger's "Being and Time"*. Berkeley: The University of California Press.

Kisiel, Theodore. (2002). "On the Way to *Being and Time*; Introduction to the Translation of Heidegger's *Prolegomena zur Geschichte des Zeitbegriffs*." In *Heidegger's Way of Thought: Critical and Interpretative Signposts*, ed. Alfred Denker and Marion Heinz, 36–63. New York: Continuum.

Kraatz, Karl. (2022a). "A New Look at *Being and Time*: Heidegger's Self-Criticism in *On My Own Publications*." *Review of Metaphysics* 75: 501–524.

Kraatz, Karl. (2022b). "Martin Heidegger's Transcendental Ontology." *Idealistic Studies* 52 (2): 133–155.

Lambeth, Morganna. (2023). *Heidegger's Interpretation of Kant: The Violence and the Charity*. Cambridge: Cambridge University Press.

Liu, Renxiang. (2024). "On the Autonomy of the Transcendental Time-Horizon: An Essay in De-Subjectivizing Heidegger's Kant-Interpretation." *Sophia* 63: 215–238.

McGrath, Sean J. (2006). *The Early Heidegger and Medieval Philosophy: Phenomenology for the God Forsaken*. Washington, DC: The Catholic University of America Press.

Polt, Richard. (2015). "From the Understanding of Being to the Happening of Being." In *Division III of Heidegger's 'Being and Time': The Unanswered Question of Being*, ed. Lee Braver, 219–238. Cambridge, MA: MIT Press.

Richardson, William J. (1967). *Heidegger: Through Phenomenology to Thought*, 2nd ed. The Hague: Martinus Nijhoff.

Rosemann, Philipp. (1996). *Omne ens est aliquid: introduction à la lecture du 'systeme' philosophique de saint Thomas d'Aquin*. Louvain: Peeters.

Rosemann, Philipp. (2015). "What Is an Author? Divine and Human Authorship in Some Mid-Thirteenth-Century Commentaries on the *Book of Sentences*." *Archa Verbi* 12: 35–65.

Schalow, Frank. (2020). "Being-Historical Thinking and the Task of Translation: Heidegger's 'Return' to Kant." *Heidegger Studies* 36: 263–278.

Schmitz, Kenneth. (2005). *The Recovery of Wonder: The New Freedom and the Asceticism of Power*. Montreal: McGill-Queen's University Press.

Searle, John. (1991). "Response to Eddy M. Zemach." In *John Searle and His Critics*, ed. Ernest Lepore and Robert Van Gulick. Cambridge, MA: Basil Blackwell.

Searle, John. (1995). *The Construction of Social Reality*. New York: Free Press.

Searle, John. (2005). "The Phenomenological Illusion." In *Erfahrung und Analyse*, ed. Maria E. Reicher and Johann Christian Marek, 317–336. Vienna: ÖBV & HPT.

Sheehan, Thomas. (2015a). "Did Heidegger Ever Finish *Being and Time*?" In *Division III of Heidegger's 'Being and Time': The Unanswered Question of Being*, ed. Lee Braver, 259–283. Cambridge, MA: MIT Press.

Sheehan, Thomas. (2015b). *Making Sense of Heidegger: A Paradigm Shift*. London: Rowman & Littlefield International.

Sokolowski, Robert. (1978). *Presence and Absence: A Philosophical Investigation of Language and Being*. Bloomington, IN: Indiana University Press.

Sokolowski, Robert. (2008). *The Phenomenology of the Human Person*. New York: Cambridge University Press.

Stein, Edith. (2002). *Finite and Eternal Being: An Attempt at an Ascent to the Meaning of Being*, tr. Kurt Reinhardt. Washington, DC: ICS Publications.

Stein, Edith. (2007). "Martin Heidegger's Existential Philosophy," tr. Mette Lebech. *Maynooth Philosophical Papers* 4 (2007): 55–98.

Stein, Edith. (2009). *Potency and Act: Studies Toward a Philosophy of Being*, tr. Walter Redmond. Washington, DC: ICS Publications.

Stein, Edith. (2014a). *"Freiheit und Gnade" und weitere Beiträge zu Phänomenologie und Ontologie (1917–1937), Gesamtausgabe* 9, ed. Beate Beckmann-Zöller und Hans Rainer Sepp. Freiburg: Herder.

Stein, Edith. (2014b). *Letters to Roman Ingarden*, tr. Hugh Candler Hunt. Washington, DC: ICS Publications.

Tate, Adam R. (2015). "On Heidegger's Root and Branch Reformulation of the Meaning of Transcendental Philosophy." *The Journal of the British Society for Phenomenology* 46: 1, 61–78.

Velkley, Richard L. (2011). *Heidegger, Strauss, and the Premises of Philosophy: On Original Forgetting*. Chicago, IL: University of Chicago Press.

Withy, Katherine. (2015). "Being and the Sea: Being as *Phusis*, and Time." In *Division III of Heidegger's 'Being and Time': The Unanswered Question of Being*, ed. Lee Braver, 311–328. Cambridge, MA: MIT Press.

Wood, Robert E. (2015a). *The Beautiful, the True, and the Good: Studies in the History of Thought*. Washington, DC: The Catholic University of America Press.

Wood, Robert E. (2015b). "The Heart in Heidegger's Thought." *Continental Philosophy Review* 48: 445–462.

Wood, Robert E. (2018). *Being and the Cosmos: From Seeing to Indwelling*. Washington, DC: The Catholic University of America Press.

Zaborowski, Holger. (2016). "Metaphysics, Christianity, and the 'Death of God'." In *Heidegger's* 'Black Notebooks' (1931–1941), ed. Ingo Farin and Jeff Malpas, 195–194. Cambridge, MA: MIT Press.

Acknowledgments

In 2024, my teacher, Monsignor Robert Sokolowski, turned ninety. A quarter of a century ago, his course on Husserl's *Logical Investigations*, delivered to celebrate the book's centenary, introduced me to the interplay of presence and absence and drew me across the threshold from boredom to wonderment – an experience that is renewed every time I slice open one of Sokolowski's many books. Was it not for his Husserl, I would not be equipped to make sense of Heidegger beyond a superficial level.

In 2024, my mentor, Richard Velkley, turned seventy-five. Two decades ago, as I tried to find my way into a dissertation topic on the question of origin in Leibniz and Heidegger, he walked to his shelves of books, pulled down Heidegger's *Die Frage nach dem Ding*, and read to me from a concluding paragraph, which concerns the "between" that emerges through transcendental reflection. "I don't believe anyone has written on that extraordinary passage," he remarked. I had a topic.

I dedicate this Element to both of them in gratitude for the path they opened up to me.

Cambridge Elements

The Philosophy of Martin Heidegger

Series Editors

Filippo Casati

Lehigh University

Filippo Casati is an Assistant Professor at Lehigh University. He has published an array of articles in such venues as The British Journal for the History of Philosophy, Synthese, Logic et Analyse, Philosophia, Philosophy Compass and The European Journal of Philosophy. He is the author of Heidegger and the Contradiction of Being (Routledge) and, with Daniel O. Dahlstrom, he edited Heidegger on logic (Cambridge University Press).

Daniel O. Dahlstrom

Boston University

Daniel O. Dahlstrom, John R. Silber Professor of Philosophy at Boston University, has edited twenty volumes, translated Mendelssohn, Schiller, Hegel, Husserl, Heidegger, and Landmann-Kalischer, and authored Heidegger's Concept of Truth (2001), The Heidegger Dictionary (2013; second extensively expanded edition, 2023), Identity, Authenticity, and Humility (2017) and over 185 essays, principally on 18th–20th century German philosophy. With Filippo Casati, he edited Heidegger on Logic (Cambridge University Press).

About the Series

A continual source of inspiration and controversy, the work of Martin Heidegger challenges thinkers across traditions and has opened up previously unexplored dimensions of Western thinking. The Elements in this series critically examine the continuing impact and promise of a thinker who transformed early twentieth-century phenomenology, spawned existentialism, gave new life to hermeneutics, celebrated the truthfulness of art and poetry, uncovered the hidden meaning of language and being, warned of "forgetting" being, and exposed the ominously deep roots of the essence of modern technology in Western metaphysics. Concise and structured overviews of Heidegger's philosophy offer original and clarifying approaches to the major themes of Heidegger's work, with fresh and provocative perspectives on its significance for contemporary thinking and existence.

Cambridge Elements

The Philosophy of Martin Heidegger

Elements in the Series

Heidegger on Being Affected
Katherine Withy

Heidegger on Eastern/Asian Thought
Lin Ma

Heidegger on Thinking
Lee Braver

Heidegger's Concept of Science
Paul Goldberg

Heidegger on Poetic Thinking
Charles Bambach

Heidegger on Religion
Benjamin D. Crowe

Heidegger and Kierkegaard
George Pattison

Heidegger on Technology's Danger and Promise in the Age of AI
Iain D. Thomson

Heidegger On Presence
Richard Polt

Heidegger on Transcendence
Chad Engelland

A full series listing is available at: www.cambridge.org/EPMH

For EU product safety concerns, contact us at Calle de José Abascal, 56–1°, 28003 Madrid, Spain or eugpsr@cambridge.org.

www.ingramcontent.com/pod-product-compliance
Ingram Content Group UK Ltd.
Pitfield, Milton Keynes, MK11 3LW, UK
UKHW022144080726
473066UK00010B/741

* 9 7 8 1 0 0 9 5 1 5 9 9 3 *